THEMATIC LEARNING ADVENTURES FOR YOUNG CHILDREN

Weekly Integrated Curriculum Units
For The Whole Year

by
Debbie Duguran
and
Margot Hopkins

Incentive Publications, Inc.
Nashville, Tennessee

Dedications

In loving memory of my father, William Henry Blair, and a special thanks to Cecilia, my daughter, for her loving encouragement.

Margot

To my mom, who always encouraged my creativity as a child and as an adult.

Debbie

Cover by Jan Keeling
Illustrated by Marta Drayton
Edited by Jan Keeling and Leslie Britt

ISBN 0-86530-283-9

PRINTED IN THE UNITED STATES OF AMERICA.

Table of Contents

HOW TO USE THIS BOOK

Thematic Learning Adventures for Young Children is a curriculum book, planned in a calendar format for the entire year. The activities are targeted for children under seven years of age in a preschool, child care center, or kindergarten setting. Each month-long chapter includes:

- A calendar
- A two-page "Parent Packet" to send home
- Background facts for each theme
- Special days
- Circle time activities
- Art activities
- Recipes for tasty treats
- Booklists
- Certificates for positive reinforcement

Also included are a growth and development observation form for the teacher and a series of self-esteem tips to be sent home to parents. By writing this book, we hope to encourage teachers to help children develop a love of self and a sense of wonder and to appreciate the joy of learning. *Thematic Learning Adventures* will help the teacher create an environment that promotes group effort, minimizes individual competition, and ensures a high degree of success for every child.

Calendar and Parent Packet

A generic calendar and two-page Parent Packet are provided at the beginning of each chapter. The calendar has two objectives: to aid teachers in lesson planning and to promote parent involvement in the curriculum. Sending copies of the calendar and packet home each month will stimulate home-school communication. The calendar can be displayed in a special place at home so that both parent and child can refer to it daily for special-day information. Parent and child can work together to discover the wonder of each day.

The calendar is full of special days with fun-filled ways to celebrate each theme. Ideas for implementing these special days are provided throughout the book. The generic calendar can be changed to fit the school's needs. The teacher may wish to cut out the squares and rearrange them (on another calendar or on a separate copy of the calendar provided) to suit the school's schedule and holidays, which will change each year. Extra days have been included at the bottom of the calendar.

The two-page Parent Packet was designed to pique parental interest in the curriculum and offers suggestions for activities which parents can do with their own children, highlighting special activities and themes. It can be sent home with the calendar each month.

Facts

Basic research has been done for the teacher; each theme is accompanied by a list of pertinent facts.

Special Days

Special days are offered for each month, along with a variety of ideas on how to implement them. A celebration of each day is a delight as children wear something to school that relates to the theme. Parent and child can enjoy sharing time together preparing for some of the activities. For example, during insect week, they can search together for an insect to share at school.

The special days are more than celebrations. They were designed to include gross motor activities, dramatic play, interactive play, and activities that enhance social skills, cognitive skills, creative thinking, self-expression, imagination, and creativity.

Circle Time

The circle time activities promote a sense of wonder and curiosity as the children explore the world around them. Included in these activities are games, group projects, and fingerplays. Lists of high-quality books that complement group time are also provided. Circle time enhances cognitive skills, social and emotional development, fine and gross motor skills, language development, creativity and self-expression, listening and thinking skills, creative thinking, self-awareness, independence, problem-solving, and learning through the five senses.

Art Activities

Art activities that allow children to experience various materials and media are provided for each theme. When implementing these activities, we emphasize the process rather than the product. Manipulating and exploring are much more important than final products. Experiencing art activities reinforces fine motor skills, imagination, creativity, self-expression, understanding of cause-and-effect, positive self-esteem, and hand-eye coordination.

Tasty Treats

Preparing and eating tasty treats contributes to the exploration of new and different foods and gives children hands-on experiences. Several cooking suggestions are given for each theme, with a weekly cooking day marked on the calendar. This day can be moved to any day of the week to accommodate the school's schedule. A cooking activity is an opportunity for children to work on mastering cooperation, taking turns, following directions, self-help skills, independence, understanding of cause-and-effect, measuring, pouring, and mixing.

List of Books

Accompanying each theme is a list of books. A selection of these books is suggested for use for circle times and special days. Books can be wonderful tools to stimulate discussions about a theme. Books allow children to grow in language development, listening, and visual skills.

Certificates

Certificates should be distributed to all children, not just a selected few. At the completion of each theme, the presentation of a certificate can help boost a child's self-esteem. Add to the certificate a personal note relating to the child's week, or to a special accomplishment, in order to individualize these special awards.

January

Theme	Monday	Tuesday	Wednesday	Thursday	Friday
Baby Animals	Share a song about an animal	Share a baby animal picture	Bring in a baby animal stuffed toy	Wear an animal on your clothes	Cooking Day: Taste different kinds of milk
Space	Meteorite Day	Earth Day: Wear blue and green	Mars Day: Wear red/share a circle	Bring in a picture of our closest star/ Star Hunt	Cooking Day: Earth Cookies
African Culture	Martin Luther King Day	Tie-Dye Day	Wear the color purple today	Learn a word in Swahili	Cooking Day: African Soup
Groundhogs and Shadows	Make shadow animals with our hands	Trace our shadows on butcher paper	Measure our shadows in the morning and afternoon	Go on a walk to find homes of animals that live underground	Cooking Day: Taste vegetables that grow underground

Extra Days

Extra Day: A surprise visit from a live baby animal	Extra Day: Wear a funny hat	Extra Day: Can you find a poem about your shadow?

Dear Parents and Caregivers,

We will ring in the new year with fresh learning adventures. January's lessons will take your small explorer from the world of baby animals to the outer reaches of the Solar System. You can share in these important days of educational play by making January's school activities a part of your child's life at home.

On _____ , send your child to school with a stuffed animal to share, and on _____ , your child may wear clothing with animal designs. This will be a good week to give some special care to an animal and practice gentle touches.

Our space explorers will love talking with you about their travels throughout the Solar System. It's easy to make the Moon and Sun out of paper and play enlightening games with your child, who will hold up the Moon or the Sun to answer a question. Ask, "When you're at school, is the Sun or Moon up?" "When you're in bed..." and so on. Or make a sweet solar system out of marshmallows (see "A Taste of Space" below). Your child will enjoy the space fingerplay "Five Little Stars." With each little disappearing star, fold down the thumb or a finger of one hand.

During our week of study of African culture, read aloud stories about Martin Luther King, Jr., and take trips through picture books that show just how fascinating African history and culture is. Remember to send an old tee-shirt for tie-dyeing on _____ .

During the last week of January, we will be preparing for Groundhog Day (February 2). We will shed some light on the subject of shadows—you can help at home by using a flashlight to demonstrate how light shines on an object, making a shadow.

Sincerely yours,

_____

A Taste of Space

Use miniature colored marshmallows for planets. Connect them with toothpicks to make them look like a solar system.

Space Fingerplay: Five Little Stars

Five little stars sitting by the door—
One went through, and then there were four.
Four little stars, as happy as can be—
One faded out, and then there were three.
Three little stars shining in the blue—
One fell down, and then there were two.
Two little stars, having so much fun—
One went home, and then there was one—
One little star, waiting for the sun.
Morningtime came, and then there were none.

Week 1: Baby Animals

Facts

- The animal kingdom is made up of living things that have the ability to move from place to place. This ability, plus a metabolism that does not use photosynthesis, distinguishes the animal kingdom from the plant kingdom.

- Animals such as reptiles who cannot control their body temperatures are known as cold-blooded. In cold weather, they become sluggish.

- Mammals and birds are warm-blooded animals. They are able to maintain a constant body temperature even in cold weather.

- Mammals are hairy animals who give live birth to their young and whose females produce milk for their babies. Human beings are mammals.

- Children will enjoy learning the names of some mother and baby animals. A few of these are: cow (calf), mare (foal), sow (piglet), hen (chick), ewe (lamb), kangaroo (joey), lioness (cub), nanny (kid), doe (fawn), [bear] sow (cub).

Special Days

Monday: During Circle Time, have children share songs about baby animals: "Farmer in the Dell," "Baa Baa Black Sheep," "Mary Had a Little Lamb," etc.

Tuesday: Children share and talk about their animal pictures. Make a baby-animal scrapbook for all the children to enjoy.

Wednesday: Have each child bring in a stuffed baby animal to share at Circle Time. Allow children to describe their special animals.

Thursday: Children come to school wearing clothing with animal designs.

Friday: Throughout the day, children can taste different kinds of milk. Try goat's milk if it is available. Other fun beverages to try are chocolate milk, strawberry milk, infant formula, low-fat milk, skimmed milk, buttermilk, etc.

Circle Time

1. Open Circle Time by reading the book *Three Kittens*. Talk about the different kinds of animals children have in their homes. Children can share stories about their pets. Follow with this fingerplay, acting out appropriate motions (holding, rocking, hand cupped behind ear, using fingers to pull mouth into a smile):

I have a kitten that I love to hold.
She cuddles with me when she gets cold.
I love to hear her purring sound.
That means she's happy, I have found.

Communication/Creative Play

2. Bring several blocks and toy animals to Circle Time. Children will build a home or a fence for the animals out of blocks or other materials and share what they have built.
   Building/Communication

3. Play a circle game in which children try to find a lost baby animal. One child leaves the group so the others can't see him or her. This child pretends to be a lost baby animal, making an animal sound so that other children can find him or her. Children try guessing the kind of animal that is lost.
   Make-believe/Identifying Animal Sounds

4. Collect several different kinds of food that animals eat. Match toy animals to the proper foods. Suggested foods are: hay, corn, carrots, bones, milk, grain, and lettuce.
   Matching Food and Animals

5. Discuss and show pictures of mother and baby animals. Let children become familiar with mother and baby names. Refer to Facts for animal names.
   Identifying Mother and Baby Animals

Art Activities

Pink Pigs: Cut out baby pigs from white construction paper. Children dip sponges in pink paint and cover the baby pigs with the paint, using light dabbing motions.

Collars: Cut out long strips of paper for each child. Have children decorate these strips with markers or crayons. Fasten with glue around child's neck to make a collar. The children may pretend to be dogs or cats.

Bone Prints: Children dip bone-shaped dog biscuits in paint and press on paper.

Tasty Treats

Animal Sandwiches: Give each child a slice of cheese and a slice of bread. Children choose animal cookie cutters to cut out their cheese and bread to make animal sandwiches. The scraps that are left over may be eaten as well.

Pigs in a Blanket: Separate canned biscuits and give one to each child to wrap around a Vienna sausage. Bake the "pigs in a blanket," following directions for baking biscuits.

Animal Standups: Spread peanut butter on graham crackers; stand animal crackers in peanut butter.

Books: Baby Animals

Animals Born Alive and Well by Ruth Heller. Putnam, 1982.

Are You My Mother? by P.D. Eastman. Random House, 1960.

Good Morning, Chick by Mirra Ginsburg. Mulberry Books, 1980.

Three Kittens by Mirra Ginsburg. Crown, 1973.

Zoo Babies by Donna K. Grosvenor. National Geographic Society, 1978.

See page 21 for Baby Animals Certificate.

Week 2: Space Facts

- Earth is the only planet in our galaxy that has an atmosphere that can support life. The Sun and the Earth were formed at about the same time, about 4.6 billion years ago. Earth is the third planet from the Sun.

- The Sun is a medium-sized star. Earth revolves around this star, the Sun.

- Mars, smaller than Earth, has red sand and polar ice caps. Because of its color, Mars is often called the Red Planet.

- Meteorites are objects from outside the Earth that enter the Earth's gravitational field and may fall to the Earth's surface, or may burn up in the atmosphere. Scientists can learn much about our Solar System from the study of meteorites.

- About 240,000 miles from Earth is the Earth's Moon. The Moon has no atmosphere; its gravitational strength is about one-sixth that of Earth.

Special Days

Monday: Make a papier maché meteorite out of paper bags and wallpaper paste or a flour-and-water mixture. Form a big ball by adding more and more paste-soaked paper bags. Dig a big hole in the sand area in which you can place the meteorite. Pretend with the children that a meteorite has fallen from the sky onto your playground. Be prepared for the gales of delighted laughter!

Tuesday: Children wear green or blue to represent the colors of the Earth. Display pictures of the Earth throughout your school.

Wednesday: Children wear red in honor of the Red Planet Mars and bring circle-shaped objects to share with the class.

JANUARY

Thursday: Pictures of the Sun are brought in by the children. Teachers hide many yellow stars and one silver star around the school or playground. Children find stars and take home the ones they find.

Friday: Make Earth Cookies (page 16).

Circle Time

1. Give each child a paper Moon and Sun. Ask questions such as "When you are at school, is the Sun or Moon up? When you are playing..." and so forth. Children hold up the Sun or Moon to answer the questions. The Moon is visible at various times of the month during daylight hours. The Sun, of course, is never visible at night. Share the book *Papa, Please Get the Moon for Me* for group closure.
   Science/Observation

2. Introduce the fingerplay "Five Little Stars" (see Parent Letter, page 11). Turn off the lights and have children make twinkling stars by turning flashlights on and off.
   Counting/Rhyme

3. Make two sets of variously-sized colored felt circles to represent the planets. Place one set of planets on the flannelboard. Children match the planets with the extra set. A good follow-up gross motor activity is to provide various sizes of balls to represent the planets. Children will pretend they are jumping over planets.
   Matching Colors and Sizes/Gross Motor

4. Show the children pictures of astronauts, planets, and space shuttles. Have the children talk about where they would like to go if they were astronauts. A record to use with this activity is Greg and Steve's "Adventure in Outer Space."
   Science/Communication

Art Activities

Spacecraft: Find a large appliance box for the spacecraft. Make a door in the box through which children can enter the vehicle. Children may decorate the spacecraft with paints, chalk, and add-ons.

Earths: Cut out large circles from tagboard. Children spread glue all over their circles, then sprinkle them with green and blue sand.

Stuffed Moons: Cut newsprint in big circles. Let children sponge-paint the circles a light gray color. When dry, take two circles and staple them together around their edges, leaving an opening to stuff with newspaper. Finish stapling the open edge and hang moons from the ceiling of your classroom.

Solar System: Children place sticky stars on black construction paper and draw the planets with colored chalk.

Tasty Treats

Earth Cookies: Using cookie cutters, children cut circles from refrigerator dough. After baking, frost cookies with green and blue colored frosting. Add food coloring to canned white frosting for color.

Solar System Sweets: Make planets with miniature colored marshmallows. Connect them with toothpicks to make them look like the Solar System.

Books: Space

Babar Visits Another Planet by Laurent de Brunhoff. Random House, 1972.

Curious George Gets a Medal by Hans Augusto Rey. Houghton Mifflin, 1957.

I Want To Be an Astronaut by Byron Barton. Crowell, 1988.

Moon Game by Frank Asch. Prentice-Hall, 1984.

Papa, Please Get the Moon for Me by Eric Carle. Scholastic, 1986.

See page 21 for Space Certificate.

Week 3: African Culture

Facts

• A clergyman and political leader, Martin Luther King, Jr., was the most prominent leader of the American civil rights movement of the 1950s and 1960s. He inspired people to deal with injustice in nonviolent ways such as sit-ins and boycotts. "I have a dream" is a quotation from one of his famous speeches. Martin Luther King, Jr., an African-American, won the Nobel Peace Prize in 1964.

• Africa is the second-largest continent. Over 800 languages are spoken by its people. Its land is covered by deserts, grasslands, and tropical rain forests. Africa is famous for its wild animals.

Special Days

Monday: Display pictures of Martin Luther King, Jr., throughout school. Have a big birthday celebration with cake and candles. Sing "Happy Birthday" to Martin Luther King, Jr.

Tuesday: Send notes home to parents several days before tie-dyeing day, reminding them to send an old tee-shirt to school with their child. Put several colors of liquid dye in separate containers. Twist rubber bands around sections of the tee-shirts and have children dip the twisted part of the shirts into the dye. Remove rubber bands, and hang out to dry.

Wednesday: Children wear purple apparel to school. Paint pictures with purple, use purple magic markers, look for purple colors in the environment, etc.

Thursday: Have fun learning some words in Swahili: baba (*bah-bah*)—father; mama (*mah-mah*)—mother; watoto (*wah-toe-toe*)—children; shule (*shoe-lay*)—school; jambo (*jahm-bow*)—hello; chakula (*cah-koo-lah*)—food.

Friday: Children can prepare African Soup and serve it for a snack or for lunch (page 18).

Circle Time

1. Show pictures of Martin Luther King, Jr., and discuss how he tried to make the world a better place. He dreamed that a day would come when all people would be treated as equals. Ask children to think of ways that they could make their school a better place.
    Values Clarification/Discussion

2. Cut small tee-shirts out of different colors of construction paper. Make different patterns on each shirt. Children can match shirts that have similar patterns.
    Recognizing and Matching Patterns

3. Bring purple objects to Circle Time (purple crayon, ribbon, barrette, comb, paper, etc.). Put objects on a tray and cover with a towel. Remove one object and ask children to guess which object is missing. Continue until all objects are gone.
    Game/Memory Skills

4. Read the story *The Land of Many Colors* written by the Klamath County YMCA Family Preschool, Klamath Falls, Oregon (Scholastic, 1983). Have children re-enact the story. Before their presentation, color a purple, blue, or green heart on each child's cheek. One child can pretend to be the child covered with dust. After the re-enactment, discuss how people of all colors can live together cooperatively, sharing with each other.
    Learning About Customs/Values Clarification

Art Activities

Tissue Shirts: Cut several shirts out of white tissue paper. Have children use eye droppers to drop colored water on their tissue-paper shirts. Display shirts by hanging on a string with clothespins.

Creative Drawing: Ask each child to create a picture of people of different colors, united in some way.

People Collage: Children cut out pictures of people of different nationalities and glue the pictures on paper to make a collage.

Tasty Treats

African Soup: In a large kettle, put 9 cups of water, 6 beef bouillon cubes, 3 diced unpeeled potatoes, 2 diced onions, 2 diced tomatoes, and ½ cup brown sugar. Cook until vegetables are tender (about 20 minutes). While soup is cooking, have children shell 2 cups of peanuts. Add peanuts for the last 10 minutes of cooking time.

Baked Sweet Potatoes: Bake sweet potatoes for about an hour at 350 degrees. Take potatoes out of skins and mash. Serve potatoes with butter.

Books: African Culture

Africa Dream by Eloise Greenfield. The John Day Company, 1977.

Bringing the Rain to Kapiti Plain by Verna Aardema. Scholastic, 1981.

Jambo Means Hello by Muriel Feelings. Dial Books, 1976.

Why Mosquitoes Buzz in People's Ears by Verna Aardema. Dial Books, 1978.

Wild Animals of Africa by Beatrice Brown Borden. Random House, 1982.

See page 22 for African Culture Certificate.

Week 4: Groundhogs And Shadows

Facts

- Groundhog Day is February 2. As legend has it, if the groundhog (woodchuck) comes out of his hole and sees his shadow, we are in for six more weeks of winter.

- The groundhog dines on vegetables and fruit. He is a vegetarian.

- A shadow is a dark image made by a body such as a groundhog or a person.

Special Days

Monday: If it is a sunny day, go outside to make hand animal shadows. If necessary, stay inside and use artificial light. Your fingers can make rabbit ears, a dog, a quacking duck, etc.

Tuesday: Tape newsprint on an outside wall or sidewalk. Trace each child's shadow on the paper. Children can color their shadows.

Wednesday: Measure children's shadows, marking them with chalk or tape. Compare morning measurements with afternoon measurements.

JANUARY

Thursday: Children delight in taking a walk, especially if they are looking for something special. It would be quite an experience for children to find the home of an animal.

Friday: Bring in vegetables that grow underground and have children taste them (see Tasty Treats below).

Circle Time

1. Make flannelboard shadow shapes of animals or people. Children can count the shadows as they are removed one by one from the flannelboard. Follow the activity with this fingerplay, adding appropriate motions:

My Shadow

I see my shadow, and my shadow sees me.
I wave to my shadow, and my shadow waves to me.
I run with my shadow, and my shadow runs with me.
I love my shadow, and my shadow loves me.

Math/Counting

2. Use a flashlight to show children how light shines on an object and makes a shadow. Conclude Circle Time by reading the book *I Have a Friend*.
Science/Light and Shadow

3. Arrange chairs to form a tunnel and cover with a sheet. Children can pretend to be groundhogs crawling through a tunnel, coming out to look for their shadows.
Creative Play

4. Ask children to think of animals that live underground, such as moles, gophers, snakes, etc. Show pictures of these animals.
Science/Animal Study

5. Encourage children to bring in newspaper clippings on or after February 2 that tell if the groundhog saw his shadow.
Research/News

Art Activities

Shadow Painting: Cut sponges in the shape of children or groundhogs. Sponge black paint on white paper.

Mud Painting: Children use mud to fingerpaint on a piece of paper.

Children's Pictures: Have each child draw a picture of a groundhog and tell a story about it.

Tasty Treats

Underground Vegetables: Taste different vegetables that grow underground, such as potatoes, carrots, onions, turnips, etc.

Groundhog Salad: Make a salad of different kinds of lettuce. Children will enjoy washing and tearing the lettuce for their salad.

Books: Groundhogs and Shadows

Bear's Shadow by Frank Asch. Prentice-Hall, 1985.

Groundhog's Day at the Doctor by Judy Delton. Parents' Magazine Press, 1981.

I Have a Friend by Keiko Narahashi. M.K. McElderry Books, 1987.

Mr. Wink and His Shadow, Ned by Ned Dick Gackenbach. Harper & Row, 1983.

What Happened Today, Freddy Groundhog? by Marvin Glass. Crown, 1989.

See page 22 for Shadow Certificate.

Baby Animals

I learned about life's new beginnings with a fun and furry exploration of baby animals!

My name is _____

SPACE

I launched into a discovery of the big wonders of outer space!

My name is _____

AFRICAN CULTURE

Back on Earth this week, I learned about the many special gifts from African culture.

My name is:
_____

Shadow

I met a new friend—

—its name is Shadow!

My name is _____

February

Theme	Monday	Tuesday	Wednesday	Thursday	Friday
Love	Bring in a picture of a loved one	Nose Painting Day	Share a doll or stuffed toy you love	Wear the color red or heart shapes today	Cooking Day: Gelatin Jiggler Hearts
Valentine's Day	Make cards for a nursing home	Pink Day: Draw a picture on the giant pink heart	Field Trip: Deliver cards to the nursing home	Valentine exchange and party	Cooking Day: Strawberry Milk
America and the Presidents	Wear red, white, and blue	Mark your birthplace on the U.S.A. map	Bring a penny to share (Whose picture is on the penny?)	Cherry Day! Taste cherries/count the cherries on our cherry tree	Cooking Day: Hot Dogs
Zoo Animals	Wear spots like a leopard	Monkeying Around Day	Zoo Animal Parade (What animal will you be?)	Wear stripes like a zebra	Cooking Day: Monkey Milkshakes

Extra Days

Extra Day: Today, forgive a friend with whom you are angry or disappointed	Extra Day: Pretend you are a child living during George Washington's presidential term	Extra Day: Cooking Day: Cinnamon Toast

Dear Parents and Caregivers,

This month at school is all heart. You'll just fall in love with all we're up to by taking part in February's exciting learning activities.

The first week introduces the importance of love as the essence of life. This is a good time for your family to encourage the sharing of feelings and to talk about the things, people, and activities you love. Write down your child's thoughts and save them for the years to come. It's a fitting way to prepare for Valentine's Day, the focus of our second week. During this time, remind your child to wear pink, and spend time talking about the trip to the hospital or nursing home where we will deliver love cards.

Mid-month, we turn our attention to America and the nation's presidents. You can help by suggesting your child wear red, white, and blue colors and by contributing a penny for your child to take to school for a counting game (we count pennies and tell the class about the president pictured on the coin). Spin a globe together and find where America is in relationship to other countries. Talk about where your child was born, and we will mark the birthplace on our map.

The month really goes wild during Zoo Animal Week. We safari through the world of the zoological garden and study creatures great and small. Your child will love wearing clothing with dot, spot, and striped designs.

When you make these February adventures a part of your home life, you create a continuum of learning that enhances your child's total experience. So join in the activities this month!

Sincerely yours,

_____

A Taste at the Zoo: Monkey Milkshakes

Blend milk, chocolate ice cream, and a banana together for a delicious milkshake.

President Fingerplay: Lincoln Head Penny

Five little pennies rolled in the door.
One was spent—now there are four.
Four little pennies belong to me.
One was lost—now there are three.
Three little pennies put in my shoe.
One bought gum—now there are two.
Two little pennies sitting on my thumb.
One fell off—now there is one.
One little penny outside, hot from the sun.
I picked it up—now there are none.

Week 1: Love

Concepts

- The essence of life is love.
- By showing children love and respect, love and respect are reflected back to you—and passed on to their peers.

Special Days

Monday: Ask each child to bring in a picture of someone he or she loves. At Circle Time, each child can share about the loved person or animal.

Tuesday: On Nose Painting Day, use a washable marker to draw a heart on each child's nose.

Wednesday: A loved doll or stuffed animal is a special visitor for this day. Display the visitors on a shelf labeled "the love shelf."

Thursday: On this special day, children wear red colors and hearts on their clothing. (Underwear, socks, and shoes count!)

Friday: In the early morning, prepare Gelatin Jiggler Hearts with the children (page 27).

Circle Time

1. Before Circle Time, cut out heart shapes in many different colors and sizes and then cut them into halves. Pass them out at random to children. During Circle Time, children will match their heart halves. Talk about the special meaning of hearts and valentines.
   Cooperation/Matching Colors and Shapes

2. Read the book *I Love You, Mouse* at the beginning of Circle Time. Ask each child to name the things or people he or she loves. Write down each child's comments and display them on the walls.
   Communication/Self-awareness

3. Place construction paper hearts in a small basket. Pass the basket around, asking each child to count out a designated number of hearts.
   Math/Counting

4. Put together a "love book." Each child should be provided a special heart page on which to draw (or write) stories of love throughout the week. This is a great book to display during the following week (Valentine week). Complete Circle Time with the

poem "I Have A Heart":

> *I have a heart, and it belongs to me.*
> *If you look inside it, you will see*
> *I have lots of love to give away,*
> *And maybe I'll give some to you one day.*

Creativity/Language Development

Art Activities

Waxed Paper Hearts: The teacher cuts heart shapes out of waxed paper and each child grates pink, red, and white crayons onto one heart. Cover with another waxed paper heart. The teacher irons the hearts with a warm iron. Display hearts on windows for a stained glass look.

Heart Necklaces: Cut out many small hearts from construction paper. Punch a hole in each heart and pass one out to each child. Children string hearts on yarn and tie around their necks to make attractive necklaces.

I Love To . . . Pictures: Using crayons or markers, children draw pictures of all the things they love to do.

Tasty Treats

Cinnamon Toast: This is a cooking activity children can do by themselves. Place a toaster, bread slices, butter, cinnamon, and sugar on a table. The children take turns toasting bread and preparing it with butter, cinnamon, and sugar. The best part is eating it. Variation: cut the bread in heart shapes before toasting.

Gelatin Jiggler Hearts: Mix four envelopes of unflavored gelatin with three packages (in the four-serving size) of flavored gelatin. Add four cups of boiling water and stir until gelatin is dissolved. Pour into 9" x 13" pan and chill until firm. Cut into heart shapes.

Books: Love

Blow Me a Kiss Miss Lilly by Nancy White Carlstrom. Harper & Row, 1990.

I Love You, Mouse by John Graham. Harcourt Brace Jovanovich, 1976.

Just Me and My Dad by Mercer Mayer. Golden Press, 1977.

Love You Forever by Robert Munsch. Firefly, 1986.

On Mother's Lap by Ann Herbest Scott. McGraw-Hill, 1972.

See page 35 for Love Certificate.

Week 2: Valentine's Day

Facts

- Valentine's Day falls on February 14th.

- The tradition of sending valentines comes from a medieval belief that birds begin to mate at the beginning of the second fortnight of the second month.

- The customary colors for Valentine's Day are white, red, and pink.

Special Days

Monday: To show caring and love for other people, children make special valentine cards for residents of a nursing home or hospital.

Tuesday: All wear the color pink on their clothes. Display a large pink heart and have children draw pictures on it.

Wednesday: Plan a field trip to a nursing home or hospital so that children can deliver their valentine love cards.

Thursday: Children bring in valentines to exchange with one another. Hide hearts throughout the school for children to find during the Valentine's Day celebration. They can take home what they find.

Friday: Make Strawberry Milk (page 29).

Circle Time

1. Have children pass a heart around the circle. As the heart comes to each child, he or she names something or someone he or she loves. Then the heart is passed to the next person. Close Circle Time with a valentine game. One child, holding a heart shape, walks around the circle and taps the head of each child, saying "Valentine." As the child walks around the circle, he or she chooses another child to be It by dropping the heart in back of the child and saying "Be my Valentine." The selected child stands up and chases the other child to the empty place in the circle.
   Self-expression/Cooperation

2. Cut out several heart shapes from tagboard. On each heart glue a different texture (sandpaper, aluminum foil, fabric, cotton balls, etc.). At Circle Time, present the hearts. Have each child pick one and describe the texture of the heart.
   Observation/Communication

3. Make big, medium, and small hearts for the flannelboard. Place Cupid or an arrow

behind one of the hearts and ask children to guess if the object is behind a big, medium, or small heart.
Following Directions/Size Recognition

4. Present the book *How Spider Saved Valentine's Day* to the children. After reading the book, put several shapes on the flannelboard or floor. Tell the children you will call out the names of the shapes. Each child should take the shape you name and place it in his or her lap.
Following Directions/Shape Recognition

5. Put a large heart shape in a "feely can" to pass around at Circle Time. Recite the fingerplay "Five Big Valentines":

> *Five big valentines from the corner drugstore;*
> *I mailed one to a friend— now there are four.*
> *Four big valentines, lovely ones to see;*
> *I mailed one to Mother— now there are three.*
> *Three big valentines, red and shiny new;*
> *I mailed one to Daddy and now there are two.*
> *Two big valentines, the best is yet to come;*
> *I mailed one to Grandma—now there is one.*
> *One big valentine, the giving's almost done;*
> *I mailed it to Grandpa, and now there are none.*

Math/Counting

Art Activities

Play Dough Hearts: Make pink or red play dough (see page 125 for directions). Cut out the play dough with cookie cutter hearts (or children can mold hearts with their hands). Let hearts dry. Children can take them home for parents to use as paperweights.

Heart People: Cut out many small and large heart shapes. Each child glues a small heart above a large heart onto a piece of paper. The children then use markers to draw faces, arms, and legs.

Heart Bracelets: Cut out many small hearts and punch a hole in each one. Children string hearts on pipe cleaners. Twist the ends of the pipe cleaners together to make bracelets.

Tasty Treats

Strawberry Milk: Put fresh or frozen strawberries in each child's glass. Children can pour milk and use a spoon to mash strawberries until the milk turns pink.

Heart Cookies: Children use cookie cutters to cut out heart shapes from refrigerator dough. Sprinkle dough with colored sugar and bake according to directions.

Books: Valentine's Day

How Spider Saved Valentine's Day by Robert Kraus. Scholastic, 1985.

The Valentine Bears by Eve Bunting. Clarion Books, 1983.

Valentine Friends by Ann Schweninger. Viking Kestrel, 1988.

Valentine Poems by Myra Cohn Livingston. Holiday House, 1987.

See page 35 for Valentine's Day Certificate.

Week 3: America And The Presidents

Facts

- The Declaration of Independence was signed in 1776. This signified America's independence from Great Britain.

- George Washington was America's first president. He is called the Father of His Country. Washington is known for his qualities of courage, good judgment, and impartiality.

- Abraham Lincoln is one of the most admired American presidents. He served as president from 1861 to 1865. Lincoln was a lawyer who was largely self-taught. Abraham Lincoln, often referred to as "Honest Abe," was very tall and sometimes wore a stovepipe hat.

- The portrait of Abraham Lincoln appears on the penny and the five-dollar bill. George Washington's portrait is on the one-dollar bill.

- President's Day commemorates both Lincoln's and Washington's birthdays. This holiday occurs in February.

Special Days

Monday: Make President's Day a patriotic day and have everyone wear red, white, and blue. Decorate the school using streamers of these three colors.

Tuesday: Mount a large map of the United States on cardboard or a cork board. The map can be displayed on an easel or wall. Children come to school prepared to share where they were born. Use large-headed pins to locate the birthplaces on the map. This activity can be extended over several weeks.

Wednesday: Encourage each child to bring in a penny to share. Compare the dates and appearance of the pennies.

FEBRUARY

Thursday: Bring in a variety of cherries for the children to taste. Prepare a large tree from construction paper. Use red sticky dots for cherries. Place a different number of cherries on the tree each day. Have children count the cherries each time you change the numbers.

Friday: Enjoy American hot dogs at snacktime (page 32).

Circle Time

1. Introduce the fingerplay "Lincoln Head Pennies." Put five pennies in a bowl or basket. Pass the container around the group and have the children count the pennies.

> *Five little pennies rolled in the door.*
> *One was spent—now there are four.*
> *Four little pennies belong to me.*
> *One was lost—now there are three.*
> *Three little pennies put in my shoe.*
> *One bought gum—now there are two.*
> *Two little pennies sitting on my thumb.*
> *One fell off—now there is one.*
> *One little penny outside, hot from the sun.*
> *I picked it up—now there are none.*

   Math/Counting

2. Bring a five-dollar bill, a one-dollar bill, and a penny to Circle Time. Tell the children about the persons pictured on the money. Allow everyone to look at and feel the money.
   History/Money

3. Look at a globe and show children where America is located. Point out where the children live.
   Social Studies/Map Skills

4. Talk to the children about the President of the United States. Tell them his name and briefly explain his job. Use the President's name throughout the week.
   Social Studies/Government

5. Gather many objects that are red, white, and blue. Present the objects and let children name and sort them by color.
   Categorizing/Color Recognition

Art Activities

Penny Rubbing: Tape a penny to the top of a table. Place a piece of paper over the penny. Rub a crayon over the penny and watch the penny appear on the paper.

President Pictures: Each child can draw a picture of the President and describe the President's job. Write these comments on the child's paper.

Flags: Cut small rectangles from white construction paper. Children can decorate rectangles with sticky stars and markers. Glue a popsicle stick on a rectangle to represent a flag.

Patriotic Fingerpainting: Fingerpaint using the colors red, white, and blue.

Tasty Treats

American Hot Dogs: Warm hot dogs and serve on buns. Serve with relish, ketchup, onions, and other condiments chosen by the children.

Bread-Shaped Flags: Cut out rectangles from white bread. Color cream cheese red and blue. Have children spread cheese on the bread rectangles to represent the flag.

Books: America and the Presidents

Just Like Abraham Lincoln by Bernard Waber. Houghton, 1964.

Washington's Birthday by Clyde Robert Bulla. Crowell, 1967.

See page 36 for America and the Presidents Certificate.

Week 4: Zoo Animals

Facts

- A zoo is a place where live animals are kept and shown to the public.
- A zoo is usually located in a public park.
- Zoos are sometimes called "zoological gardens."
- Among the animals frequently found in the zoo are elephants, lions, tigers, bears, giraffes, seals, monkeys, gorillas, zebras, ostriches, alligators, flamingoes, and reptiles.

Special Days

Monday: Children come to school wearing spotted clothes. Paint spots on faces, hands, and arms so that children look like leopards for the day.

Tuesday: Children pretend to be monkeys. Hang pictures of monkeys around the room. Feed your monkeys bananas and peanuts today. Encourage children to do special tricks on the monkey bars. Be sure to read the book *Gorilla*.

FEBRUARY

Wednesday: Each child pretends to be a particular zoo animal. Parade throughout the school as each animal makes its special noise.

Thursday: Striped clothing is the apparel for the day. Have the children count the stripes on their clothing and on the clothing of others.

Friday: Make Monkey Milkshakes for snacktime (page 34).

Circle Time

1. Draw and cut out a large leopard. Put it up on the wall next to the Circle Time area. Have children place a specified number of dots on the leopard (use sticky dots or cut out your own dots). Children will enjoy counting the dots all week.
   Math/Counting

2. Show pictures of zoo animals and discuss each one with the children. Allow each child to choose an animal and tell a story about that animal. Display stories with the pictures for parents and visitors to read.
   Creative Storytelling

3. Play Zoo Charades: a child pretends to be a zoo animal and the others try to guess the animal that is being acted out.
   Drama/Creative Play

4. Bring a stuffed animal monkey or elephant to Circle Time. Ask each child to feed the animal a specified number of peanuts. Change the number with each child.
   Math/Counting

5. Make a large construction paper tree and five monkeys. Recite "Five Little Monkeys Swinging from a Tree." Children take turns taking monkeys off the tree. For added fun, place a paper alligator by the tree.
   Action Rhyme/Counting

Art Activities

Molding Zoo Animals: Children mold clay into various animal shapes.

Peanut Shell Collage: Children glue peanut shells on paper to create a collage.

Zebra with Stripes: Cut zebras out of white construction paper. Cut thin strips out of black construction paper. Children glue black strips on zebras.

Tasty Treats

Zoo Popcorn: Pop popcorn and put it into small brown bags to be distributed to the children. Pretend it is popcorn from the zoo.

Monkey Milkshakes: Blend milk, chocolate ice cream, and a banana together for a delicious milkshake.

Peanuts: Children shell peanuts and eat them at snacktime.

Books: Zoo Animals

Five Little Monkeys Jumping on the Bed by Eileen Christelow. Clarion Books, 1989.

Gorilla by Anthony Browne. Random House, 1983.

Who Wants a Cheap Rhinoceros? by Shel Silverstein. Macmillan, 1964.

Zebra by Caroline Arnold. Morrow, 1987.

The Zoo That Grew by James Kruss. Platt & Munk, 1968.

See page 36 for Zoo Animals Certificate.

I showed love to Someone this week.

LOVE

My name is:_____

Valentine's Day

I spread joy and showed the importance of caring this week.

My name is:_____

AMERICA AND THE PRESIDENTS

I celebrated the birthdays of George Washington and Abraham Lincoln and learned about our presidents.

My name is:
_____

ZOO ANIMALS

I studied creatures great and small and learned what's happening at the zoo.

My name is: _____

March

Theme	Monday	Tuesday	Wednesday	Thursday	Friday
Growing Things	Make a flower arrangement	Plant a garden	Grow beans in paper towels	Wear something with a flower on it	Cooking Day: Vegetable Soup
Spring Weather	Bring in something white like a cloud	Share something that protects you from the rain	Blue Day	Bring in pictures of a cloud, the sun, or the rain	Cooking Day: Hot Yellow Suns
St. Patrick's Day	Magical Leprechaun Day	Rainbow Day: Wear the colors of the rainbow	Search for gold	Shamrock Hunt: How many shamrocks will you find?	Cooking Day: Green eggs and ham with green apple juice/wear green
Celebration of New Life	Wear a pastel color	Bunny Hop Day: Bring in a stuffed bunny to share	Easter Bonnet Day (and a parade to show off the bonnet)	Coloring eggs	Easter Egg Hunt: Eat Marshmallow Bunny Salads

Extra Days

Extra Days: March comes in like a lion and out like a lamb/ pretend to be lions and lambs	Extra Days: Explore flowers on a walk. How do they smell?	Extra Days: Celebrate Spring by pretending to be your favorite tree

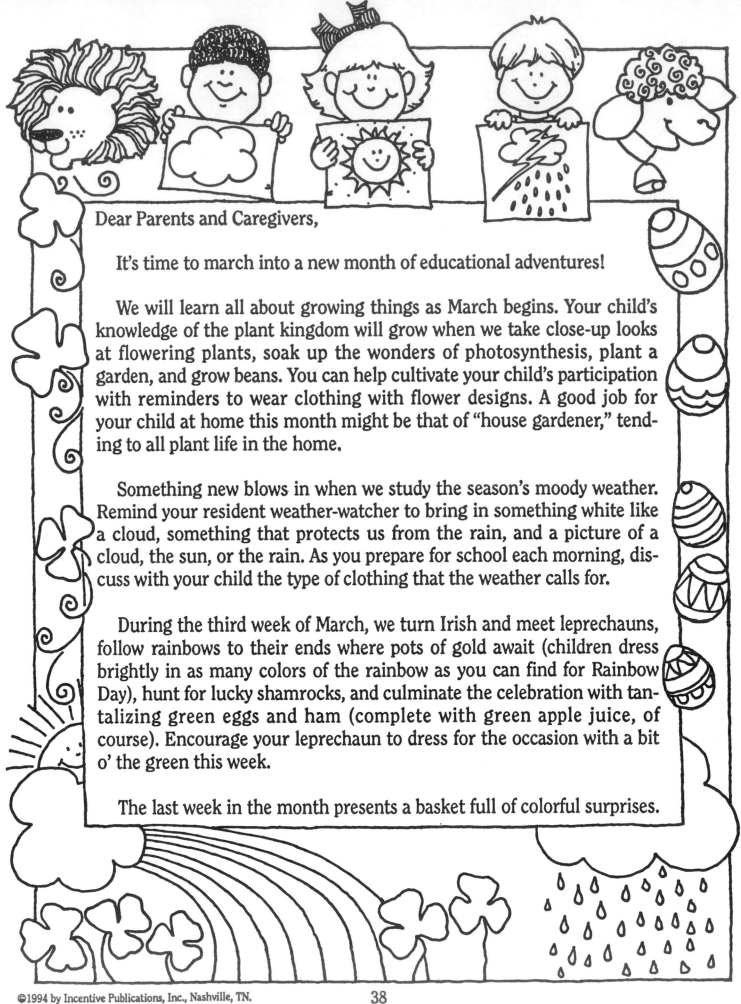

Dear Parents and Caregivers,

It's time to march into a new month of educational adventures!

We will learn all about growing things as March begins. Your child's knowledge of the plant kingdom will grow when we take close-up looks at flowering plants, soak up the wonders of photosynthesis, plant a garden, and grow beans. You can help cultivate your child's participation with reminders to wear clothing with flower designs. A good job for your child at home this month might be that of "house gardener," tending to all plant life in the home.

Something new blows in when we study the season's moody weather. Remind your resident weather-watcher to bring in something white like a cloud, something that protects us from the rain, and a picture of a cloud, the sun, or the rain. As you prepare for school each morning, discuss with your child the type of clothing that the weather calls for.

During the third week of March, we turn Irish and meet leprechauns, follow rainbows to their ends where pots of gold await (children dress brightly in as many colors of the rainbow as you can find for Rainbow Day), hunt for lucky shamrocks, and culminate the celebration with tantalizing green eggs and ham (complete with green apple juice, of course). Encourage your leprechaun to dress for the occasion with a bit o' the green this week.

The last week in the month presents a basket full of colorful surprises.

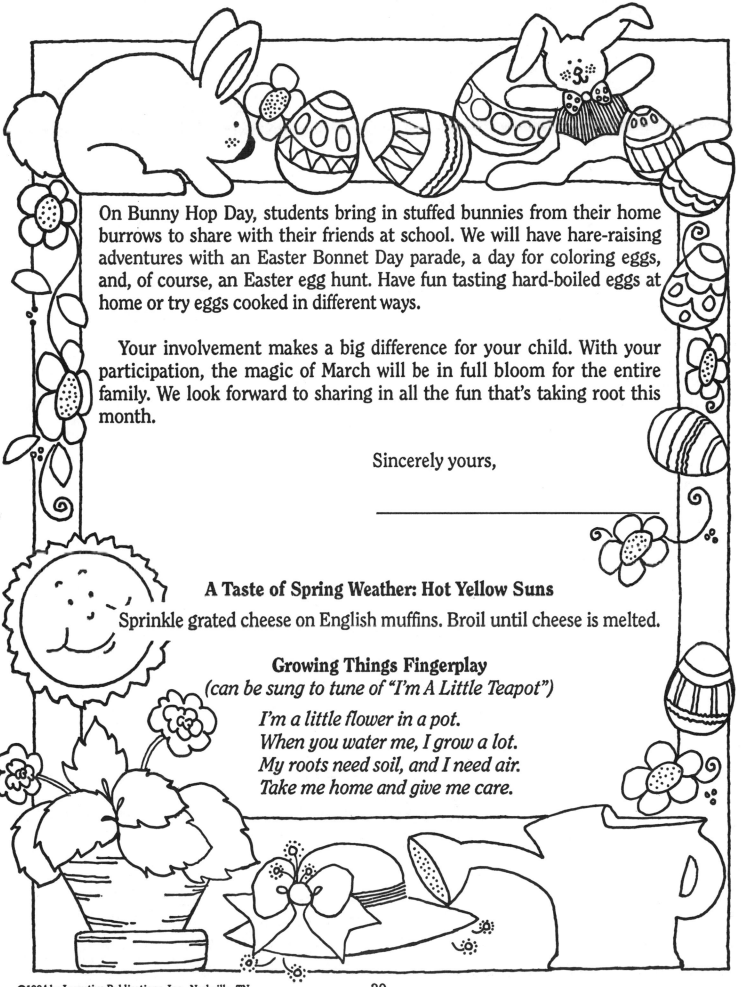

On Bunny Hop Day, students bring in stuffed bunnies from their home burrows to share with their friends at school. We will have hare-raising adventures with an Easter Bonnet Day parade, a day for coloring eggs, and, of course, an Easter egg hunt. Have fun tasting hard-boiled eggs at home or try eggs cooked in different ways.

Your involvement makes a big difference for your child. With your participation, the magic of March will be in full bloom for the entire family. We look forward to sharing in all the fun that's taking root this month.

Sincerely yours,

_____

A Taste of Spring Weather: Hot Yellow Suns
Sprinkle grated cheese on English muffins. Broil until cheese is melted.

Growing Things Fingerplay
(can be sung to tune of "I'm A Little Teapot")

I'm a little flower in a pot.
When you water me, I grow a lot.
My roots need soil, and I need air.
Take me home and give me care.

Week 1: Growing Things

Facts

- The plant kingdom is one of the five kingdoms of living things.

- Most green plants use energy from sunlight to carry out chemical reactions. This process is called photosynthesis.

- The sugars that feed the plant are produced by photosynthesis.

- The structure of a flowering plant includes a root system, stem, and leaves.

- Reproductive organs are contained in flowers, which produce seeds and fruits. These reproductive organs are the stamen (male) and pistil (female).

- The pollen of a flower grows in the stamen.

Special Days

Monday: Provide each child with a small amount of clay. Present a variety of artificial flowers for children to choose from. Arrange flowers in the clay.

Tuesday: Plant a mixture of vegetables and flowers in a garden plot outside. In a cooler climate, plant your garden inside in a wooden box. When weather gets warmer, transplant the garden outside.

Wednesday: Place a moist paper towel in a glass jar. Slip beans between paper towel and jar. Children can watch the beans sprout. Spray water into jar occasionally to moisten towel. You can make one for each child or use a large jar for the whole class to see.

Thursday: Celebrate growing things by wearing something with a flower on it. If children don't wear a flower, give them a flower sticker to put on their clothing.

Friday: Cook vegetable soup today (page 41) and read the story *Growing Vegetable Soup*.

Circle Time

1. Provide a variety of seeds for the children to touch and smell. Show children the pictures of the seed packages along with the seeds. This allows them to see what each seed will become.
   Observation/Cause and Effect

2. Draw a diagram of a flower, labeling all of its parts. Discuss these words with the children. They will delight in these new words. Learn a new fingerplay, "I'm A Little Flower" (see Parent Packet, page 39).
   Science/Vocabulary

3. Share the book *The Plant Sitter* at Circle Time. At the beginning of the week, bring in a small plant for each child. During the week, have the children water and care for their plants and name them. Children can take their plants home at the end of the week and continue to care for them.
Literature/Growing Plants

4. Talk about growing things. Ask children for ideas. Some ideas include people, plants, flowers, animals, trees, hair, fingernails, grass, and weeds.
Science/Living Things

5. Discuss the elements that plants, trees, and flowers need to live (water, air, soil, sun). Ask the children to name the things they need to live.
Science/Living Things

Art Activities

Seed Collage: Use the seeds from Monday's Circle Time. Have the children glue them onto paper. Also use the pictures from the seed packages for the collage.

Plant Story: Each child designs his or her own picture of growing things. Then ask him or her to tell you a story about the picture.

Muffin Cup Flowers: To design flowers, children glue muffin cups on paper. They can use crayons or markers to draw stems and grass.

Cucumber Printing: Cut cucumbers in half and have children dip them in green paint and press them onto white paper.

Tasty Treats

Lion Salad: Place half an apricot on a lettuce leaf. Sprinkle coconut around apricot to make the lion's mane. Use raisins to make the face.

Vegetable Soup: Everyone can participate in the soup preparation by bringing in a vegetable from home. Children prepare the vegetables and drop them into a pan of water. For added flavor, mix in 2 chicken bouillon cubes. Simmer until vegetables are tender (approximately 30 minutes).

Bean Sprouts: Children sprinkle bean sprouts on rice cakes.

Books: Growing Things

The Carrot Seed by Ruth Krauss. Harper & Row, 1945.

Growing Vegetable Soup by Lois Ehlert. Harcourt Brace Jovanovich, 1987.

The Plant Sitter by Gene Zion. Harper & Row, 1959.

MARCH

The Rose in My Garden by Arnold Lobel. Scholastic, 1984.

The Tiny Seed by Eric Carle. Crowell, 1970

See page 49 for Growing Things Certificate.

Week 2: Spring Weather

Facts

- Spring begins in the middle of March and ends in the middle of June.

- In the Spring, plants begin to grow again after the long Winter months. Trees start to bud and bloom.

- People plant gardens, trees, and other living plants in the springtime.

- Spring brings warmer weather after the cold Winter.

- There are three basic cloud formations: cirrus, cumulus, and stratus.

- Cirrus clouds are composed of ice crystals. They are wispy, white clouds high in the sky.

- Cumulus clouds are seen on nice days. These clouds are white and fluffy in appearance.

- Stratus clouds are low-hanging and spread in layers. These clouds become fog if they are resting on the ground.

- Steady rain or snow usually falls from clouds called nimbostratus. These cloud formations are dark gray stratus clouds. Thunderstorms are large cumulonimbus formations that produce sudden heavy rain, wind, thunder, and lightning.

Special Days

Monday: All bring white objects to school to share. Lie on the grass outside to observe the shapes of clouds. This is a good day to read the book *It Looked Like Spilt Milk*. Play soft music and children can pretend to be clouds floating in the sky.

Tuesday: Encourage children to bring in items that protect them from the rain.

Wednesday: Wear blue, the color of the sky. Paint pictures with blue paint and display the pictures throughout the school.

Thursday: During Circle Time, children can share their pictures of the clouds, sun, or rain. Encourage them to tell stories about their pictures.

Friday: Make Hot Yellow Suns today (page 44).

Circle Time

1. Make construction paper puddles for children to sit on during Circle Time. After Circle Time, children can arrange the puddles in a maze and jump from puddle to puddle.
   Pretending/Gross Motor Activity

2. Discuss with children how we dress when the weather begins to get warmer. Talk about the way we dress when it rains. Make a paper doll with appropriate Spring clothing. Children dress the doll and tell the group what the weather is like for the day. This is a good activity to carry through the rest of the week.
   Weather/Clothing

3. Display several cloud formations on the flannelboard. Go around the circle and ask the children what the clouds look like to them. One may look like a rain cloud, another like a pear, another like a face. Take the children outside to look at real clouds. Ask them what they see in the clouds. Allow their imaginations to soar. Teach the new fingerplay "Five Little Clouds":

   > *Five little clouds floating in the sky—*
   > *One saw a bird and wanted to fly.*
   > *Four little clouds floating in the sky—*
   > *One saw a friend and went to say "Hi."*
   > *Three little clouds floating in the sky—*
   > *One was sad and started to cry.*
   > *Two little clouds floating in the sky—*
   > *One saw the bright sun and said, "My, oh my."*
   > *One little cloud alone in the sky*
   > *Went to find the others and said, "Bye bye."*

   Imaginative Thinking/Fingerplay

4. Play "weather forecaster" at Circle Time. Each day, have one child draw a picture of the weather and tell about what the weather is like that day. For added realism, bring a microphone for children to use.
   Weather/Imaginative Play

Art Activities

Stormy Day: Cut out lightning bolts, dark storm clouds, and raindrops from construction paper. Glue these on blue paper to create a storm. For an additional activity, have children relate stories about the storm. Write their stories on the paper and display on the walls.

Clouds: Dip cotton balls into white paint and dab onto blue paper.

Yellow Suns: Cut cake-pan-sized circles out of construction paper. Place paper in a cake pan with yellow paint and a few marbles. Children make a sun by "marble painting."

Tasty Treats

Hot Yellow Suns: Sprinkle grated cheese on English muffins. Broil until cheese is melted.

Cloud Gelatin: Follow directions on gelatin package, coloring it blue with food coloring and adding miniature marshmallows to represent the clouds.

Books: Spring Weather

The Cloud Book by Tomie dePaola. Holiday House, 1975.

Hi, Clouds by Carol Greene. Children's Press, 1983.

It Looked Like Spilt Milk by Charles Green Shaw. Harper & Row, 1947.

Rain by Peter Spier. Doubleday & Co., 1982.

Spring by Richard L. Allington. Raintree Children's Books, 1981.

See page 49 for Spring Weather Certificate.

Week 3: St. Patrick's Day

Facts

- St. Patrick's Day is celebrated on March 17th.
- The color green is worn on St. Patrick's Day in honor of Ireland.
- The shamrock is a St. Patrick's Day symbol.
- The elves, called leprechauns, are told about in Irish folklore. They are shoemakers who have hidden treasure.

Special Days

Monday: Magical Leprechaun Day can be filled with silly games, glitter, and gold. During the day, children take off their shoes, and a leprechaun hides them around the playground. Children will have fun looking for their hidden shoes.

Tuesday: Decorate the school in rainbow colors. Wear a rainbow of colors on clothes. Provide rainbow colors for painting time today.

Wednesday: Make gold pieces out of paper or tagboard. Leprechauns hide the gold and children search for gold pieces.

MARCH

Thursday: Display shamrocks throughout the school so that children can become familiar with the shape. Cut out shamrocks from green construction paper. Hide shamrocks in unusual places for children to find. Also look for clover in your grass.

St. Patrick's Day: The St. Patrick's Day celebration is scheduled for Friday; rearrange this week's schedule, of course, if it falls on another day. Children wear green so that they won't get pinched. Prepare green eggs and ham and serve with green apple juice (page 46). Read *Green Eggs and Ham* by Dr. Seuss.

Circle Time

1. Read the book *The Rainbow Goblins* before the following Circle Time activity. Design a rainbow and copy it so that each child in your group will have one. Cut the colors of the rainbow out of colored paper in an arched shape to fit on each rainbow. During Circle Time, call out the color you wish each child to fit on his or her rainbow.
   Following Directions/Color Recognition

2. Make big, medium, and small gold coins out of colored paper. Display coins on a flannelboard or in the center of the group. Ask each child to pick up a big, medium, or small coin and put it in his or her lap.
   Following Directions/Size Recognition

3. Play Shamrock Shake. Each child receives a paper shamrock. Children hold shamrocks in hand and follow instructions ("shake your shamrock high, low, behind you, in front of you, etc."). Recite the poem "Shamrocks 1, 2, 3," using the paper shamrocks for counting:
   > *How many shamrocks do you see?*
   > *Let's count the shamrocks 1, 2, 3.*

   Following Directions/Counting

4. Ask the children where they would hide their pots of gold if they were leprechauns. Write down their responses and display for all to see.
   Thinking Skills/Creative Expression

5. Conduct a leprechaun game. Children stand in a circle; one child is the leprechaun. Sing to the leprechaun, "Leprechaun, leprechaun, what can you do?" The leprechaun then jumps, claps, sticks out tongue, etc., and everyone follows the leprechaun. Each child will have the chance to play the leprechaun.
   Game/Gross Motor Activity

Art Activities

Rainbow Pictures: Color water with food coloring using the colors of the rainbow. Children paint with colored water on white paper or coffee filters.

Rainbow Painting: Provide paints in the colors of the rainbow. Give each child a sheet of waxed paper and let the children use cotton-tipped swabs to paint rainbows. Hang on windows when dry.

Tasty Treats

Green Eggs and Ham: Crack eggs into a frying pan with pieces of ham. Add green food coloring to mixture and cook.

Green Apple Juice: Add green food coloring to apple juice and stir.

Shamrock Cookies: Use a shamrock-shaped cookie cutter to cut out shamrocks from refrigerator dough. Top with green sprinkles. Follow directions on package for baking.

Books: St. Patrick's Day

Green Eggs and Ham by Dr. Seuss. Random House Beginner Books, 1960.

The Rainbow Goblins by Ul de Rico. Thames and Hudson, 1978.

A Rainbow of My Own by Don Freeman. Viking Press, 1966.

St. Patrick's Day in the Morning by Eve Bunting. Houghton Mifflin, 1980.

Skyfire by Frank Asch. Scholastic, 1984.

See page 50 for St. Patrick's Day Certificate.

Week 4: Celebration Of New Life

Facts

- It is customary at this time of the year to celebrate the rebirth of nature and new beginnings.

- Easter is a Christian Holiday. It celebrates the Resurrection of Christ. Easter is observed on the first Sunday following the full moon that occurs on or after March 21st.

- The Jewish holiday Passover is celebrated for eight days in late March or early April. It celebrates God's deliverance of the Hebrew people from slavery in Egypt. Passover is observed according to the Jewish calendar and occurs from the 15th to the 22nd in the Jewish month of Nisan.

Special Days

Monday: Wear pastel colors associated with the Easter season.

Tuesday: As children arrive in the morning, dress them up like bunnies. Make bunny ears, tape on cotton balls for tails, and draw bunny whiskers on their faces with a fine point marker. Immediately, children are transformed into bunnies and hop everywhere. Before naptime, read the book *Bunnies and their Hobbies*. Children can nap with their stuffed bunnies.

Wednesday: Children make Easter bonnets (page 48). Play the music "Easter Parade" and walk around sporting the new Easter bonnets.

Thursday: Color hard-boiled eggs with a mixture of food coloring, water, and 1 teaspoon vinegar per color.

Friday. Hide the colored eggs. Conduct an egg hunt in the school yard. Prepare a Marshmallow Bunny Salad (page 48) for each child to eat at snacktime.

Circle Time

1. Make or purchase a mother hen puppet. Cut out eggs from paper of several different colors. The mother hen asks children to hand her the red, green, or blue eggs, or those of other colors. Children love putting the eggs in the puppet's mouth.
   Following Directions/Color Recognition

2. Design an egg match game. Cut out ten paper eggs. Put five pairs of Spring stickers on the eggs. During Circle Time, children match the eggs that display like stickers.
   Game/Matching

3. Prepare an Easter basket full of plastic eggs. Place a different shape in each egg. Children pick an egg and name the shape inside. Place plastic eggs in an open area. Children take turns hopping with a basket, grabbing a certain number of eggs, and hopping back.
   Shape Recognition/Counting/Gross Motor Activity

4. Make bunnies, lambs, and chicks for the flannelboard. Ask children questions such as "Which animal has long ears?" "Which animal has wool?" "Which animal has a beak?" It is fun to end this Circle Time with the rhyme "Little Peter Rabbit Had a Fly Upon His Nose." (Sing it to the tune of "The Battle Hymn of the Republic.")

   > *Little Peter Rabbit had a fly upon his nose,*
   > *Little Peter Rabbit had a fly upon his nose,*
   > *Little Peter Rabbit had a fly upon his nose,*
   > *And he flipped and he flopped and it flew away.*

   Animal Characteristics/Rhyme

Art Activities

Baby Chicks: Glue yellow cotton balls on paper. Children draw beaks and legs with magic markers. Small wiggly eyes can be added. For eggs that have not yet hatched, glue on white paper ovals.

Egg Painting: Children paint rocks as if the rocks were Easter eggs. When rocks dry, place them in egg cartons for children to take home.

Pastel Painting: Pour several colors of pastel paint into an egg carton. Children dip their paintbrushes into the egg carton and paint.

Easter Bonnets: Cut the middles out of paper plates. Use a hole punch to make holes for a ribbon tie. Decorate with dried flowers, buttons, ribbons, etc.

Tasty Treats

Easter Bonnets: Give each child a canned peach half on a paper plate. Provide several condiments for the children to use to decorate their bonnets. Some suggestions: red hots, sprinkles, raisins, nuts, and coconut.

Marshmallow Bunny Salad: Make a fruit salad, adding purchased marshmallow bunnies. Make sure each child gets a bunny in his or her salad.

Books: Celebration of New Life

Bunnies and their Hobbies by Nancy Carlson. Viking Penguin, 1984.

The Chocolate Rabbit by Maria Claret. Barron's, 1984.

The Easter Bunny by Winifred Wolf. Dial Books, 1986.

It's Not Easy Being a Bunny by Marilyn Sadler. Random House, 1983.

The Runaway Bunny by Margaret Wise Brown. Harper & Row, 1942.

See page 50 for Celebration of New Life Certificate.

I know how a garden grows and now have a green thumb.

My name is: _____

GrowingThings

Spring

I learned about Spring weather, clouds, rain, and the sun.

My name is: _____

Weather

St. Patrick's Leprechaun Magic

I celebrated the
Irish magic in
St. Patrick's Day and
met lucky leprechauns.

Name: _____

Celebration of New Life

I became a bunny, decorated and
found eggs, and showed off my
very own Easter bonnet.

My name is: _____

_____

April

Theme	Monday	Tuesday	Wednesday	Thursday	Friday
Firefighters and Police	Hat Day	Fire engine visit	Bike patrol	Police visit	Cooking Day: Licorice Hoses
Dental Health	Brushing practice	Tooth Fairy visit	Lost tooth hunt	Dentist visit	Cooking Day: Big Mouths
Nurses and Doctors	Weighing and measuring	Dress in white like doctors and nurses	Bring in a stuffed animal that needs care	Nurse visit	Cooking Day: Chicken noodle soup
Circus	Clown Day	Inside Out Day	Circus acts	Wear funny shoes	Cooking Day: Snow cones

Extra Days

Extra Day: Celebrate children's book day on April 2 by sharing a book with us	Extra Day: Bring in a song to share	Extra Day: Wear polka dots

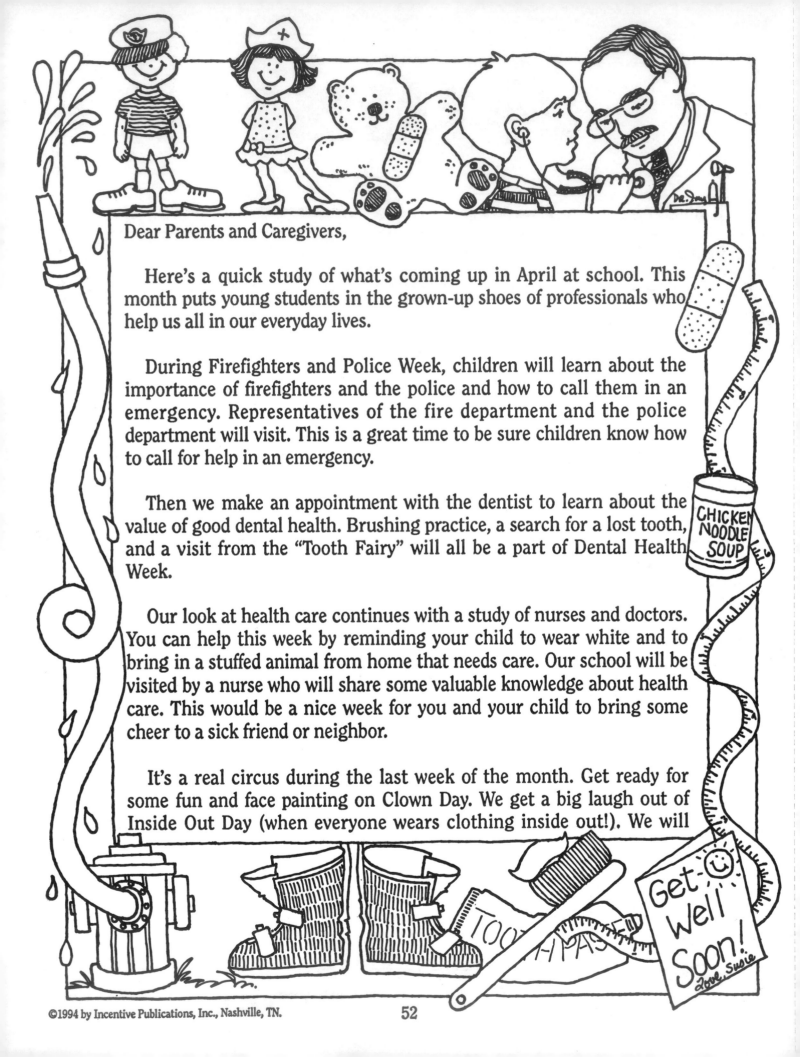

Dear Parents and Caregivers,

Here's a quick study of what's coming up in April at school. This month puts young students in the grown-up shoes of professionals who help us all in our everyday lives.

During Firefighters and Police Week, children will learn about the importance of firefighters and the police and how to call them in an emergency. Representatives of the fire department and the police department will visit. This is a great time to be sure children know how to call for help in an emergency.

Then we make an appointment with the dentist to learn about the value of good dental health. Brushing practice, a search for a lost tooth, and a visit from the "Tooth Fairy" will all be a part of Dental Health Week.

Our look at health care continues with a study of nurses and doctors. You can help this week by reminding your child to wear white and to bring in a stuffed animal from home that needs care. Our school will be visited by a nurse who will share some valuable knowledge about health care. This would be a nice week for you and your child to bring some cheer to a sick friend or neighbor.

It's a real circus during the last week of the month. Get ready for some fun and face painting on Clown Day. We get a big laugh out of Inside Out Day (when everyone wears clothing inside out!). We will

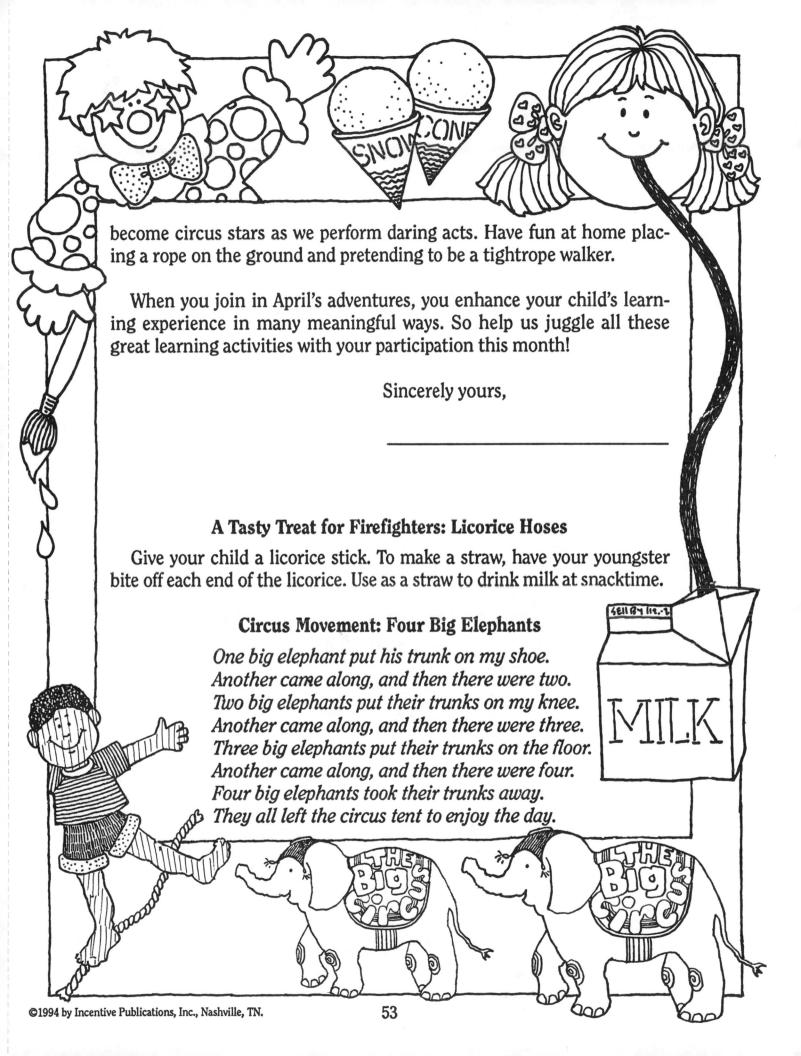

become circus stars as we perform daring acts. Have fun at home placing a rope on the ground and pretending to be a tightrope walker.

When you join in April's adventures, you enhance your child's learning experience in many meaningful ways. So help us juggle all these great learning activities with your participation this month!

Sincerely yours,

_____

A Tasty Treat for Firefighters: Licorice Hoses

Give your child a licorice stick. To make a straw, have your youngster bite off each end of the licorice. Use as a straw to drink milk at snacktime.

Circus Movement: Four Big Elephants

One big elephant put his trunk on my shoe.
Another came along, and then there were two.
Two big elephants put their trunks on my knee.
Another came along, and then there were three.
Three big elephants put their trunks on the floor.
Another came along, and then there were four.
Four big elephants took their trunks away.
They all left the circus tent to enjoy the day.

Week 1: Firefighters And Police

Facts

- Most communities have some form of fire protection service. Cities have the most elaborate equipment. Many smaller communities rely on volunteer firefighters.

- A police officer is a member of the police force in most cities and towns. The officer's job is to try to keep peace and order in the community.

- The telephone number 911 is the emergency number to dial if you ever need to reach the police, firefighters, or paramedics.

Special Days

Monday: Each child chooses a special hat to wear, such as the hat of a firefighter, police officer, or baseball player. Hats can be provided in the dramatic play area.

Tuesday: Make prior arrangements to have a fire engine visit school. Follow up on the firefighters' visit by reading the book *A Visit to the Fire Station*. Ask the children to find in the book all the equipment they saw during the firefighters' visit.

Wednesday: Make traffic vests out of paper bags. Children take turns pretending to be police officers and motorists. Each police officer receives a notepad and pen to write tickets for fun.

Thursday: Make prior arrangements for a police officer to visit school.

Friday: Prepare Licorice Hoses for snacktime (page 55).

Circle Time

1. Make a large construction paper fire truck and several paper dalmatian dogs (put dots on the dogs). On a wall, post the fire truck with the dalmations inside. Children pick a dog out of the truck and count the dots.
   Math/Counting

2. Recite the fingerplay "Firefighter," shown below, and then pass around a firefighter hat. As each child puts on the hat, he or she will name something a firefighter does or has.

   I put out fires with my hose.
   When the bell rings, I throw on my clothes.
   When a building's burning, I get people out.
   If you need help, just give me a shout!

   Firefighter Knowledge/Vocabulary

3. Design a simple maze on a large piece of newsprint. Children pretend to be lost and find their way through the maze to the police station using their index fingers. You can also play "lost child" by asking one child to hide; the other children will pretend to be police searching for the missing child.
Thinking Skills/Imaginative Play

4. Cut out the shape of a police officer's badge for each child in the group. Print the children's names on the badges. During Circle Time, pass out badges, asking children to try to recognize their names. This activity can be practiced throughout the week.
Name Recognition

Art Activities

Shape Fire Trucks: Cut out rectangles, squares, and circles from white construction paper. Children glue shapes on paper to represent fire trucks.

Fire Truck Red: Cut out a fire truck shape from white construction paper. Sponge paint the shape with red paint.

Police Cars: Roll the wheels of toy cars in paint, and then drive them over paper to make tire tracks.

Tasty Treats

Licorice Hoses: Each child receives a licorice stick, bites off each end of the stick, and uses it as a straw to drink milk at snacktime.

Firefighter Sundae: Spoon frozen or fresh strawberries on top of nonfat yogurt.

Books: Firefighters and Police

Clifford's Good Deeds by Norman Bridwell. Fourwinds Press, 1975.

My Dog Is Lost! by Ezra Jack Keats and Pat Cherr. Crowell, 1960.

Paddy's New Hat by John S. Goodall. Atheneum, 1980.

A Visit to the Fire Station by Dotti Hannum. Regensteiner Publishing Enterprises, 1985.

See page 63 for Firefighters and Police Certificate.

Week 2: Dental Health

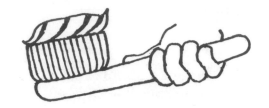

Facts

- A dentist's job is to provide care for teeth. The dentist fills cavities, replaces missing teeth, pulls teeth that are beyond repair, and teaches good dental hygiene.

- Teeth are used for chewing food. They are bone-like structures with roots, crowns, and a neck.

- Babies usually begin to get their first teeth by the time they are six to nine months old. A complete set of baby teeth numbers 20. Around the age of six or seven, children begin to lose their baby teeth and permanent teeth replace the lost set. The complete set of permanent teeth numbers 32.

Special Days

Monday: Attach each child's name to a toothbrush you have purchased for each one. Children can practice brushing their teeth properly. At the end of the week, children take their brushes home. While brushing, sing "Brush, Brush, Brush Your Teeth" to the tune of "Row, Row, Row Your Boat."

> *Brush, brush, brush your teeth,*
> *Brush them every day.*
> *Brush them high and brush them low,*
> *Brush them every way.*

Tuesday: Call your local health department to set up a visit from the "Tooth Fairy." If the department does not provide this service, have someone dress up as the Tooth Fairy and talk to the children about dental health.

Wednesday: Cut out a large tooth from white construction paper. Pretend that someone has lost the tooth and have the children try to find it. For added fun, put a cavity on the tooth with a marker.

Thursday: Make prior arrangements to have a pediatric dentist visit your school. Read the story *Just Going to the Dentist.*

Friday: Serve Big Mouths for snacks (page 57).

Circle Time

1. Place dental floss, toothbrush, toothpaste, toothpick, etc., on a tray. Allow children time to study the objects and then cover the objects with a towel. Remove objects one at a

time, and then remove towel. Children guess each time which object has been removed.
Visual Perception/Memory

2. Bring waxed and unwaxed dental floss to Circle Time. Show children the proper way to use the floss. Children practice flossing their teeth, choosing waxed or unwaxed floss.
Dental Hygiene

3. Prepare cards, each with a tooth drawn on it. One card's tooth should have a cavity. Pass out cards to children, face down. The child who receives the tooth with the cavity gets to name a way that teeth can be cared for (brush, floss, eat healthful food, etc.).
Game/Dental Hygiene

4. Draw a large face with a big mouth on posterboard. Cut out white teeth from construction paper. Draw a shape on or apply a colored sticky dot to the back of each tooth. Place sticky tabs on the posterboard mouth and on the back of each tooth. Each child "pulls" a tooth and names the color or shape on the back of that tooth.
Color/Shape Recognition

Art Activities

Toothbrush Painting: Use toothbrushes as painting tools. Green, blue, or white paint will resemble toothpaste.

Tooth Collage: Cut various sizes of teeth from white paper. Children glue teeth on paper to make a collage. Cavities can be added with black or gray markers.

Draw Your Smile: Children draw their smiles on blank pieces of paper. Ask children to tell you about their smiles.

Tasty Treats

Big Mouths: Cut red apples into wedges. Two wedges per serving will be arranged to look like a mouth. Spread peanut butter on one side of each wedge. Push miniature marshmallows into peanut butter to look like teeth.

Corn on the Cob: Cut corn into small pieces. Cook in boiling water until tender. Not only does corn look like teeth, children use their teeth to eat corn on the cob.

Books: Dental Health

The Berenstain Bears Visit the Dentist by Stan and Jan Berenstain. Random House, 1981.

I Know a Dentist by Naomi Barnett. Putnam, 1977.

Just Going to the Dentist by Mercer Mayer. Western Publishing Co., 1990.

APRIL

Teach Me About the Dentist by Joy Berry. Children's Press, 1986.

Timothy Tiger's Terrible Toothache by Jan Wahl. Western Publishing Co., 1988.

See page 63 for Dental Health Certificate.

Week 3: Nurses And Doctors

Facts

- A Doctor of Medicine's job is to treat and heal patients. Doctors go to school many years to learn their profession. Often it takes eight years or longer to become a Doctor of Medicine.

- Nurses tend the sick and injured. They work in many different places, but we most often think of them as working in hospitals. Nurses also work in schools, corporations, and private homes.

- Young children often go to the doctor when they are not feeling well. The doctor checks ears, noses, and throats, and listens to chests (lungs) to diagnose an illness or condition. A doctor will guide us on procedures to follow so that we can feel well again.

Special Days

Monday: Scales and tape measures can be brought in by children or supplied by the school. Weigh and measure each child and write the information down so each child can share his or her height and weight with parents at the end of the day.

Tuesday: Children and teachers wear white to resemble the apparel worn by doctors and nurses.

Wednesday: Children bring in stuffed animals that need first aid or medical attention. Each child can tell about the special attention his or her animal requires. Bandages and slings can be provided.

Thursday: Make prior arrangements with a hospital in your area to send a nurse to talk to the children.

Friday: Prepare chicken noodle soup (page 59).

Circle Time

1. Begin Circle Time with the fingerplay "Five Little Monkeys Jumping on the Bed." After the fingerplay, share objects a doctor uses (tongue depressor, stethoscope, blood

pressure cuff, thermometer, rubber syringe, etc.). Pass objects around and talk about their uses. Display these objects with other miscellaneous objects and a doctor's bag. Children select an object and decide if it should go in the doctor's bag or not.

Five Little Monkeys Jumping on the Bed

Five little monkeys jumping on the bed—
One fell off, and bumped his head.
Mama called the doctor and the doctor said,
"No more monkeys jumping on the bed!"
Four little monkeys . . . etc.
Three little monkeys . . . etc.
Two little monkeys . . . etc.
One little monkey jumping on the bed—
He fell off and bumped his head.
Then there were no more monkeys to jump on the bed.

Doctor's Tools/Counting

2. Talk with the children about how nurses take care of their patients. Children try to think of all the helpful things they could do for a person who is sick.
   Creative Thinking

3. Draw the outline of a child on newsprint. Each child applies an adhesive bandage to a part of the body of the newsprint child and then tells a story about how the child became hurt.
   Imagination/Storytelling

4. Reading the book *Going to the Doctor* is a great way to begin Circle Time. Each child listens to his or her own heartbeat using a stethoscope and then describes how the heart sounds.
   Literature/Communication

Art Activities

Cotton Ball Painting: Dip cotton balls into pans of paint and dab cotton balls onto paper.

Shaving Cream Play: Squirt some shaving cream onto an easel or tabletop. Children use tongue depressors to spread it around.

Tasty Treats

Chicken Noodle Soup: Simmer noodles in chicken broth until they are tender. Serve in small bowls.

Heart Toast: After toasting bread, cut it with a heart-shaped cookie cutter. Color margarine red with food coloring and have children spread it on their heart-shaped toast.

Books: Nurses and Doctors

The Berenstain Bears Go to the Doctor by Stan and Jan Berenstain. Random House, 1981.

Doctor Shawn by Petronella Breinburg. Thomas Y. Crowell Co., 1974.

Going to the Doctor by Fred Rogers. Putnam, 1986.

I Can Be a Nurse by June Behrens. Children's Press, 1986.

My Doctor by Harlow Rockwell. Macmillan, 1973.

See page 64 for Nurses and Doctors Certificate.

Week 4: Circus

Facts

- A circus is usually a traveling show. The arena is often enclosed in a large tent, auditorium, or colosseum. Most circuses have three rings in which the performers can act.

- A circus show often consists of wild animals, clowns, trapeze artists, acrobats, a ring master, and parades.

- Ringling Brothers, Barnum and Bailey is the best known circus. It was once the largest circus performed beneath a tent, but now they perform in a large auditorium or colosseum.

Special Days

Monday: Arrange to have a clown visit the classroom. Have fun painting the children's faces like clowns. Decorate the school or your classroom with balloons and streamers to make it a festive day.

Tuesday: Everyone comes to school with their clothes worn inside out.

Wednesday: Design an arena for the circus performers by making a circle with a jump rope or masking tape. Children can pretend to be elephants, bears, tight-rope walkers, clowns, etc.

Thursday: During Circle Time, have each child share their crazy shoes. Provide crazy or funny shoes for those children who are unable to bring them in for this activity.

Friday: Crunch snow cones during snacktime (page 62).

Circle Time

1. Draw a large circus tent on a piece of butcher paper, and secure it to the wall. Pretend with children that you are going to the circus. Ask them which acts and animals they will see inside the large circus tent. After discussing the exciting circus events they intend to see, have them draw on the butcher paper their imagined circus events. A good group closure is the traditional fingerplay "Four Big Elephants":

   > *One big elephant put his trunk on my shoe.*
   > *Another came along, and then there were two.*
   > *Two big elephants put their trunks on my knee.*
   > *Another came along, and then there were three.*
   > *Three big elephants put their trunks on the floor.*
   > *Another came along, and then there were four.*
   > *Four big elephants took their trunks away.*
   > *They all left the circus tent to enjoy the day.*

   Imaginative Play/Counting

2. Make a large outline of a circus clown on butcher paper. Select several colors of construction paper and cut out hats of various colors for the clown. Children secure the hats on the clown's head, relating the color of the hats they have chosen.
   Color Recognition/Communication

3. Hold out a hula-hoop and have children pretend to be tigers jumping through the hoop. They can also count how many tigers jump through the hoop.
   Gross Motor Activity/Counting

4. Place a rope across the floor. Children walk on the tightrope, moving forward, backward, sideways, etc. Ask children how many other ways they can walk. Complete Circle Time by reading *Curious George Goes to the Circus*.
   Gross Motor Activity/Following Directions

Art Activities

Funny Face: Cut out circles from construction paper. Children fingerpaint clown faces on their circles. They can glue yarn on the faces for hair.

Elephants: Cut elephant shapes from sponges. Whip soap flakes with water and add gray paint to the mixture. Children can dip the elephant sponges into the mixture and sponge onto white paper to make elephant shapes.

Polka-Dotted Clowns: Cut out a clown shape from construction paper. Children place colored sticky dots all over the clown shape to make a polka-dotted clown.

Trapeze: Cut straws into small pieces. String a piece of yarn through each straw piece. Children glue their yarn and straw pieces onto pieces of paper to look like a trapeze. They may draw in a person on the trapeze.

Tasty Treats

Snow Cones: Use an ice crusher or blender to crush ice. Pour fruit juice over ice. Serve in small bowls or paper cones.

Circus Pretzels: Use frozen bread dough and pinch off a piece for each child. Children knead and mold their bread into pretzel shapes. Place pretzels on a cookie sheet, brush with water, and then sprinkle with salt. Cook at 425 degrees for 10 to 15 minutes.

Books: Circus

The Circus Baby by Maud Petersham. Macmillan, 1950.

Curious George Goes to the Circus edited by Margaret Rey and Alan J. Shalleck. Houghton Mifflin, 1984.

If I Ran the Circus by Dr. Seuss. Random House, 1956.

Paddington at the Circus by Michael Bond. Random House, 1973.

You Think It's Fun To Be a Clown! by David A. Adler. Doubleday, 1980.

See page 64 for Circus Certificate.

Firefighters and Police

I learned how firefighters and police make my world a safer place, and I know how to call on them in an emergency.

My name is: _____

SGT. JOHN
METRO POLICE

DENTAL HEALTH

I brushed up on how to take good care of my teeth during Dental Health Care Week.

SMILE MAKER TOOTHPASTE

My name is:

_____

Nurses and Doctors

My name is: _____

I learned about what nurses and doctors do in the field of medicine.

Circus

I joined the circus and clowned around all week.

My name is: _____

May

Theme	Monday	Tuesday	Wednesday	Thursday	Friday
Cinco De Mayo	Learn some Spanish words today	Hit the piñata/wear the colors of the Mexican flag	Grand Parade Day	Mexican Hat Dance	Cooking Day: Mexican food tasting
Insects	Wear green like a grasshopper	Bring an insect to share	Wear the colors of a ladybug	Take a trip to the park to find insects	Cooking Day: Ants on a Log
Spiders	Spider Crawl	Bring in a picture of a spider	Wear black like a spider	Spider Web-Making Day	Cooking Day: Spider Salad
Honeybees	Wear yellow and black like a honeybee	Bee Hunt: How many bees can you find at school today?	Dress in stripes like a bee	Honey Tasting Day	Cooking Day: Lemonade with honey

Extra Days

Extra Day: Bird Watching Day	Extra Day: Make May baskets	Extra Day: Bring in a May flower

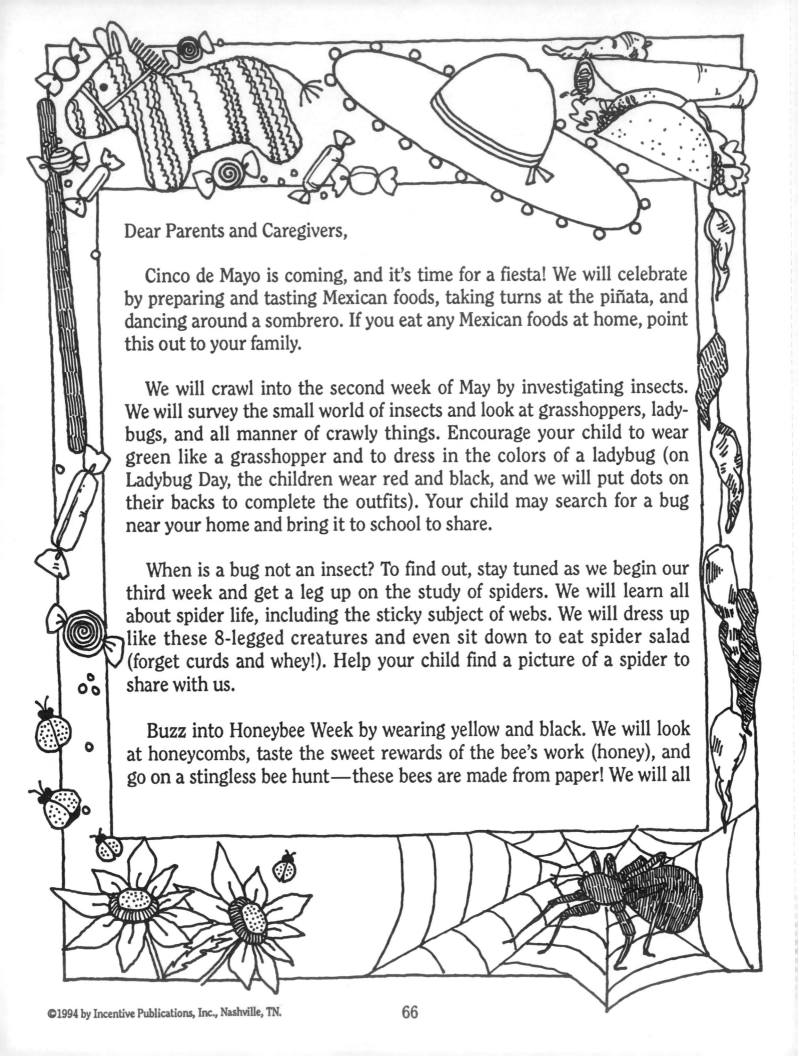

Dear Parents and Caregivers,

Cinco de Mayo is coming, and it's time for a fiesta! We will celebrate by preparing and tasting Mexican foods, taking turns at the piñata, and dancing around a sombrero. If you eat any Mexican foods at home, point this out to your family.

We will crawl into the second week of May by investigating insects. We will survey the small world of insects and look at grasshoppers, ladybugs, and all manner of crawly things. Encourage your child to wear green like a grasshopper and to dress in the colors of a ladybug (on Ladybug Day, the children wear red and black, and we will put dots on their backs to complete the outfits). Your child may search for a bug near your home and bring it to school to share.

When is a bug not an insect? To find out, stay tuned as we begin our third week and get a leg up on the study of spiders. We will learn all about spider life, including the sticky subject of webs. We will dress up like these 8-legged creatures and even sit down to eat spider salad (forget curds and whey!). Help your child find a picture of a spider to share with us.

Buzz into Honeybee Week by wearing yellow and black. We will look at honeycombs, taste the sweet rewards of the bee's work (honey), and go on a stingless bee hunt—these bees are made from paper! We will all

look like bees when we come dressed in stripes. Back at your family's hive, have a honey-filled treat by tasting honey-flavored cereals.

Sincerely yours,

_____

Spider Salad: A Tasty Spider Treat

Place a prune on a lettuce leaf. Use pretzel sticks for legs and raisins for eyes.

Honeybee Fingerplay: Little Bee

One little bee, flying in the sky so blue,
Sat beside another bee, and then there were two.
Two little bees, buzzing around a tree—
Another bee joined them, and then there were three.
Three little bees, wishing there were more—
Along came another bee, and then there were four.
Four little bees, glad to be alive,
Found a little friend, and then there were five.
Five little bees, just as happy as can be.
Five little bees, making honey for you and me.

Week 1: Cinco De Mayo

Facts

- Cinco de Mayo (Spanish for fifth of May) is a patriotic fiesta which celebrates Mexico's triumph in the Puebla battle on May 5, 1862. Mexico gained its independence from France at this time.

- A grand parade is held on one of Mexico City's boulevards on Cinco de Mayo.

- The colors of the Mexican flag are red, green, and white.

- The culture of Mexico is a combination of Hispanic and Indian traditions.

Special Days

Monday: Introduce Spanish greetings such as *buenos dias, buenos noches, buenos tardes,* etc. Expand vocabulary throughout the week by introducing other familiar Spanish sayings or counting from one to ten in Spanish.

Tuesday: Have children take turns hitting a piñata filled with popcorn, raisins, and peanuts. Dress in the colors of the Mexican flag, which are red, green, and white.

Wednesday: Stage a grand parade by decorating tricycles with crepe paper streamers and having children carry red, green, and white streamers.

Thursday: Children dance around a sombrero. A good song to play while children dance is "Cinco de Mayo" from Hap Palmer's album *Holiday Songs and Rhythms.*

Friday: Prepare and taste a variety of Mexican foods (see page 69 for suggestions).

Circle Time

1. Share artifacts from Mexico (dolls, pottery, jewelry, clothing, etc.). Pass the objects around the classroom for the children to hold and touch.
   Multicultural Study/Mexican Artifacts

2. Share agricultural products from Mexico (cotton, coffee, wheat, and sugar cane, for example). Allow children to smell and touch products.
   Multicultural Study/Mexican Agricultural Products

3. Show and discuss a map of Mexico.
   Mexico/Map Skills

4. Show pictures of the Mexican countryside and the people who live there. Suggested resources for pictures are National Geographic magazines and postcards. Each child then chooses a picture representing some aspect of Mexico and tells a story about the picture. The teacher can write down the students' stories and display them throughout the week.
Multicultural Study/Mexico and Its People/Storytelling

5. Bring a tortilla to Circle Time and discuss with the children the kinds of foods that might be used to make a burrito. Each child can take turns being wrapped in a large white sheet to represent a burrito and rolled down a small hill.
Mexico/Gross Motor Activity

Art Activities

Maracas: Fill two small paper plates with dried beans. Staple the plates together and paint the outsides of the plates green or red.

Piñata: Inflate a balloon. Dip newspaper strips in a mixture of glue and water. Stick the strips on the inflated balloon, allow them to dry, and then decorate with streamers and paint.

Clay Pots: Children use modeling clay or play dough to mold their own clay pots.

Streamers: Staple red, green, and white crepe paper streamers to an empty brightly-painted toilet paper roll.

Tasty Treats

Guacamole: Mash ripe avocados. Add chopped tomatoes, onions, and lemon juice. Serve dip with tortilla chips.

Taco Salad: Brown hamburger. Mix with lettuce, shredded cheese, diced tomatoes, onions, and tortilla chips.

Tostadas: Spread refried beans on a tostada shell. Sprinkle with shredded cheese, diced tomatoes, and green chilies.

Books: Cinco de Mayo

Carlos Goes to School by Eloise A. Anderson. F. Warne, 1973.

Maria by Joan Lexau. Dial, 1964.

MAY

Mario's Mystery Machine by Sibyl Hancock. Putnam, 1972.

See page 77 for Cinco de Mayo Certificate.

Week 2: Insects

Facts

- While insects are many different shapes and sizes, all insects have 6 legs and 3 body parts (the head, thorax, and abdomen).
- All insects also have antennae for detecting odors and touch.
- Spiders are not insects; they have only 2 body parts.

Special Days

Monday: Encourage children to wear green like a grasshopper today.

Tuesday: Children bring in insects to share with the class. Create a special place in the classroom in which to display the bugs.

Wednesday: Encourage children to wear red and black, the colors of the ladybug. Children can also wear clothing with dots, as ladybugs have black spots on their backs. *The Grouchy Ladybug* is a perfect book to read today.

Thursday: Take a trip to a park to catch insects. Before leaving for the field trip, make Milk Carton Bug Catchers (see page 71 for directions). Have each child take his or her insect catcher to the park and collect bugs with it.

Friday: Allow each child to make Ants on a Log (page 72).

Circle Time

1. A great way to begin each day's Circle Time this week is by reading the riddle "Fly." Have children lie on their backs and pretend to be a fly walking on the ceiling. Ask children how it would feel to be a fly.

Fly

He tickles my nose and lands on my toes.
When I'm eating lunch, he is there with a bunch.

He lands on my food and walks around.
When he flies he makes a buzzing sound.
This little guy can walk on walls—
And you know what? He never falls!
Who is this?

Imagination/Poetry

2. Make a bug maze by taping masking tape to the floor in various patterns. Have children crawl through the maze.
   Gross Motor Activity/Navigating a Maze

3. Draw a giant bug on a piece of posterboard and hang it on a wall. Each day, each child should sign his or her name or make a special mark on the bug's body.
   Recordkeeping/Writing Name

4. Children share bugs from the bug hunt and tell stories about the bugs they caught.
   Insects/Storytelling

5. Draw a giant ant on newsprint and attach the ant to the wall. Have children draw small paper ants. The children move the paper ants around the classroom and other rooms and discuss how the ants might use these rooms to complete their daily activities.
   Science/Ants

Art Activities

Lady Bugs: Paint half a walnut shell red and let it dry. Add black spots and glue on small wiggly eyes (available at most craft stores).

Milk Carton Bug Catchers: Cut the top off of a milk carton. After catching bugs and placing them in the carton, cover the top of the carton with a piece of nylon hose and secure it with a rubber band. Let bugs go after sharing.

Insects: Mix equal parts of flour and water in a bowl. Children dip cotton balls into the mixture and place the balls on a foiled cookie sheet. Once on the cookie sheet, pipe cleaners can be added to represent legs. Bake in an oven for 15 minutes at 350 degrees, or until hard.

Ant Hill: Have children draw ant hills after discussing how they look and their function.

Tasty Treats

Bug Cookies: Use refrigerator cookie dough. Have children drop dough shaped like bugs onto cookie sheets. The tops of the cookies can be painted with a mixture of evaporated milk and food coloring. Bake until done.

MAY

Ants on a Log: Spread peanut butter on celery sticks and top with raisins to represent ants.

Books: Insects

The Grouchy Ladybug by Eric Carle. Harper Collins, 1977.

How To Hide a Butterfly and Other Insects by Ruth Heller. Grosset & Dunlap, 1985.

Inch by Inch by Leo Lionni. Astor-Honor, 1960.

Sam and the Firefly by P.D. Eastman. Random House, 1958.

The Very Quiet Cricket by Eric Carle. Philomel Books, 1990.

See page 77 for Insects Certificate.

Week 3: Spiders

Facts

- Spiders are not insects. They have only 2 body parts (the cephalothorax and the abdomen) whereas insects have 3 body parts. Spiders also have no wings or antennae.

- Spiders have 8 legs.

- Spiders eat the bodily juices of insects, which they hunt or trap in their webs.

- Spiders are known for the beautiful webs they weave. Most spiders spin their webs from silk threads produced by glands in their bodies.

- The spider's prey is wrapped in bands of silk before being killed by its poison fangs. The insect's bodily fluids are then sucked out by the spider.

Special Days

Monday: Children pretend to be spiders and crawl to recess, to Circle Time, to tables for snacktime, etc.

Tuesday: Children bring in pictures of spiders to share during Circle Time.

Wednesday: Have children dress in black to resemble spiders. During the day, decorate the room with black streamers and paint paper with black paint.

Thursday: Have children make a giant spider web on the floor using yarn. This is a good day to have fun marble painting (see Spider Web, page 73).

Friday: Make Spider Salad (page 74).

Circle Time

1. Draw spider webs on tagboard squares, approximately 5 inches by 5 inches. Number the squares 1 through 5, and draw corresponding dots on the squares for children who cannot read numbers. Allow children to put the appropriate number of plastic spiders on the webs.
   Math/Number Recognition/Counting

2. Place a toy spider in your feely box or can. Have children touch it and try to guess what it is. You may want to read Eric Carle's book *The Very Busy Spider* and recite a favorite fingerplay:

   The Eensy, Weensy Spider

   The eensy, weensy spider went up the water spout.
   Down came the rain and washed the spider out.
   Out came the sun and dried up all the rain.
   And the eensy, weensy spider went up the spout again.
   (Repeat, using daddy, mommy, or baby spider.)

   Literature/Fingerplay

3. Attach a string spider web to the corner or wall of your room. Each day, children can attach different plastic insects to the web. Children can also attach plastic spiders. If available, bring a live tarantula for children to observe throughout the week.
   Science/Spider Study

4. Draw several large geometrical shapes on a piece of tagboard. Have children place plastic spiders on the various shapes as you call them out.
   Following Directions/Shape Recognition

Art Activities

Spider Web: Place black paper in a box with sides or edges. Drop a small amount of white paint and two marbles on the paper. Each child shakes the box to make a web design.

Egg Carton Spiders: Cut out each egg cup from an egg carton. Pass out the egg cups to the children and have them paint each cup black. Add pipe cleaners for legs and wiggly eyes (available at craft stores).

Creative Spider Walk: Children draw pictures of a spider taking a walk. For example, the spider can walk under a car, on a sidewalk, up a tree, etc. Upon completing their drawings, children discuss their spiders' walks.

Tasty Treats

Spider Salad: Place a prune on a lettuce leaf. Use pretzel sticks for legs and raisins for eyes.

Cheese Webs: Children design spider webs using string cheese. Raisins can be used to represent spiders in the webs.

Books: Spiders

The Very Busy Spider by Eric Carle. Philomel Books, 1984.

See page 78 for Spiders Certificate.

Week 4: Honeybees

Facts

- There are 20,000 known species of bees in the world.
- Bees live entirely on the pollen and nectar of flowers.
- Honey is made from the nectar which bees gather little by little from many different flowers. Once gathered by the bees, this nectar is then regurgitated by the bee into the cells of the hive.
- The honeybee lives in a highly organized society.
- The honeybee is an important creature because it helps to pollinate crops.

Special Days

Monday: Encourage children to dress as bees by wearing yellow and black clothing today.

Tuesday: Make paper bees and hide them throughout your school. Children hunt for the bees and take home the ones they find.

Wednesday: Encourage children to dress in stripes like bees today.

Thursday: If available, bring in a honeycomb. If no honeycombs are available, bring in a jar of honey for the children to taste. For an added sensory experience, have the children feel the consistency and texture of the honey.

Friday: Make lemonade with honey (page 76).

Circle Time

1. Begin Circle Time with the fingerplay "Little Bee." Have children finish the sentence: "If I were a bee, I would. . ."

Little Bee

One little bee, flying in the sky so blue,
Sat beside another bee, and then there were two.
Two little bees, buzzing around a tree—
Another bee joined them, and then there were three.
Three little bees, wishing there were more—
Along came another bee, and then there were four.
Four little bees, glad to be alive,
Found a little friend, and then there were five.
Five little bees, just as happy as can be.
Five little bees, making honey for you and me.

Imaginative Thought/Counting

2. Make paper bees of various colors and place them in an envelope. Pass around the envelope to the group of children and ask each child to remove a bee of a specified color and place it behind, in front, to his or her left or right, etc.
Color Recognition/Following Directions

3. Take children on a walk to count bees. Ask children to listen to the sounds that bees make and watch them take nectar from the flowers.
Science/Bees

4. Draw the cells of a beehive on tagboard. Using plastic or paper bees, have children pretend to draw nectar from flowers and take it back to their cells. If desired, add a queen bee to the hive.
Imaginative Play/Bees

Art Activities

Cereal Art: Glue honey-flavored cereal onto paper. Paper bees can be added to the art or children can draw bees on the paper.

Painting: Children paint using yellow and black colors.

Flowers: Glue muffin cups onto paper to make flowers. Green paper stems can be added and bees drawn to complete the picture.

Bracelets: Make bracelets by stringing honey-flavored cereal on pipe cleaners.

Tasty Treats

Lemonade with Honey: Squeeze the juice of half a lemon into a glass. Add a cup of water and a tablespoon of honey.

Oatmeal with Honey: Prepare instant oatmeal and use honey as a sweetener. Accompany this tasty treat with the nursery rhyme "Little Miss Muffet," pretending that the oatmeal is curds and whey.

Books: Honeybees

Buzz, Buzz, Buzz by Byron Barton. Macmillan, 1973.

See page 78 for Honeybees Certificate.

June

Theme	Monday	Tuesday	Wednesday	Thursday	Friday
Farm Life	Wear a red bandanna	Pink Pig Day	Bring in something that grows on a farm	Corn husking and tasting	Cooking Day: Piggies in a Blanket
Farm Life	A scarecrow will visit	Wear brown and black like horses and cows	Cheese tasting and cheese art	County Fair: Visit our exports	Cooking Day: Omelettes
Teddy Bears	Wear a teddy bear on your clothing, or wear brown like a bear	"The Three Bears": Drama	Share a teddy bear poem or book	Teddy Bear Picnic: Invite your teddy bear	Cooking Day: Root Bear Floats
Summer Weather	Sunshine Day	Swimsuit and Waterplay Day	Wear a summer hat or visor	Beach Party: Bring in a sand pail	Cooking Day: Popsicles
Extra Days	Extra Day: Fly a kite	Extra Day: Wear the color of your favorite bear	Extra Day: Bring in a water toy to share		

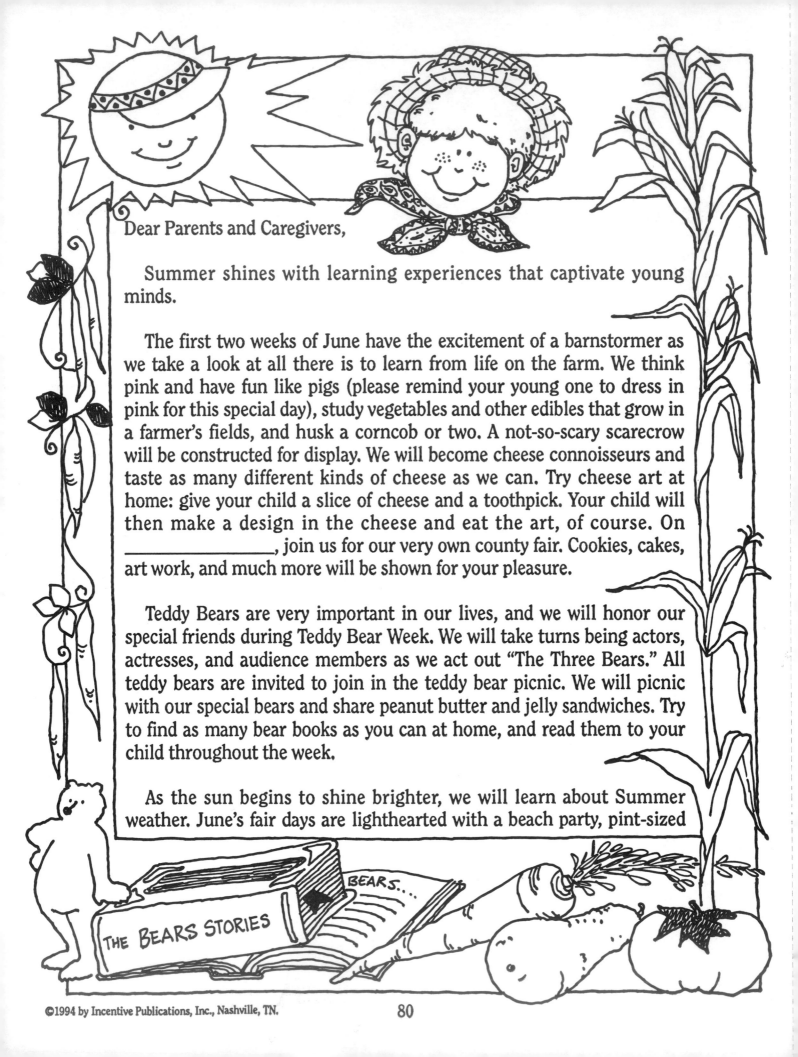

Dear Parents and Caregivers,

Summer shines with learning experiences that captivate young minds.

The first two weeks of June have the excitement of a barnstormer as we take a look at all there is to learn from life on the farm. We think pink and have fun like pigs (please remind your young one to dress in pink for this special day), study vegetables and other edibles that grow in a farmer's fields, and husk a corncob or two. A not-so-scary scarecrow will be constructed for display. We will become cheese connoisseurs and taste as many different kinds of cheese as we can. Try cheese art at home: give your child a slice of cheese and a toothpick. Your child will then make a design in the cheese and eat the art, of course. On _____, join us for our very own county fair. Cookies, cakes, art work, and much more will be shown for your pleasure.

Teddy Bears are very important in our lives, and we will honor our special friends during Teddy Bear Week. We will take turns being actors, actresses, and audience members as we act out "The Three Bears." All teddy bears are invited to join in the teddy bear picnic. We will picnic with our special bears and share peanut butter and jelly sandwiches. Try to find as many bear books as you can at home, and read them to your child throughout the week.

As the sun begins to shine brighter, we will learn about Summer weather. June's fair days are lighthearted with a beach party, pint-sized

water play with swimsuits (remind your child to dress for the occasion), the chilling delight of ice cream, and other summery sensations.

So bask in the rays of new educational experiences with your child during the month of June. We look forward to the bright days ahead.

Sincerely yours,

_____

A Taste of Teddy Bears: Root Bear Floats
Place a scoop of ice cream in a glass. Pour root beer over the ice cream.

Farm Life Song: "I'm a Little Piglet"
(to the tune of "I'm a Little Teapot")

I'm a little piglet who loves to play;
In the mud all day I will stay.
My tail is curly, any food I will take;
Oink, oink, oink is the noise I make.

Week 1: Farm Life

Facts

- Machinery replaced animal and hand labor on most farms at the beginning of the 20th century. There are still some farms today, however, that use horse-drawn plows.

- Some machines used on farms include tractors, combines, wheat cutters and binders, cotton pickers, tractor-drawn plows, and potato planters—just to mention a few!

- State and county fairs aid in developing unity among farmers. Fairs allow farmers to exhibit their agricultural products such as livestock, vegetables, wheat, and other grains. There are also exhibits of such household products as canned goods, clothing, quilting, and needlework. Educational displays are usually part of state and county fairs as well. Fairs are typically festive events, and carnivals and other forms of entertainment are often available at the fair.

- The most common livestock on farms are cows, sheep, pigs, chickens, and horses.

- Farmers play a very important role in our society. They provide us with an abundance of food and other resources upon which we depend daily.

Special Days

Monday: Gallop into the first week of farm life by wearing red bandannas.

Tuesday: Decorate the school with pink pigs cut from construction paper. Arrange a special display area for stuffed pink pigs brought in by the children. Pink clothing can also be worn today.

Wednesday: A variety of agricultural products can be brought in today. Have fun with eggs, corn, broccoli, potatoes, wheat, cotton, cheese, milk, butter, yogurt, and alfalfa.

Thursday: Purchase corn in husks. Allow children to husk the corn and feel and smell the corn husks and silks. Cut the corn cobs into small pieces, boil until tender, and eat.

Friday: Pig out on Piggies in a Blanket (page 83).

Circle Time

1. Draw a large farmyard and barn on newsprint. Attach to a wall at a height the children can reach. Each day, children can draw something new that they have learned about farm life on the drawing.
   Farm Life/Storytelling/Drawing

2. Place yellow cotton balls in a container. Pretend that they are baby chicks and ask children to count out a specified number of chicks.
Math/Counting

3. Make a horse, cow, pig, and lamb for the flannelboard. Place the animals on the flannelboard and ask the children: "Which animal has a curly tail?" "Which animal says moo?" "Which animal has wool?" "Which animal can be ridden?" etc.
Flannelboard/Farm Animals

4. Show pictures of horses to the group. Discuss with children how they think horses are used on the farm. Ask them how they would like to be horses on a farm.
Farm Life/Horses

Art Activities

Corn Printing: Roll a corn cob into yellow paint and across a piece of construction paper to make a corn print.

Clay Pigs: Children mold clay into pig shapes. Pink pipe cleaners can be stuck in the clay to make curly tails.

Farm Life Collage: Place several magazines on a table in the classroom. Children tear or cut out from the magazines pictures of farm life and glue them onto separate pieces of paper.

Tasty Treats

Piggies in a Blanket: Wrap canned biscuits around Vienna sausages. Bake according to directions on biscuit package.

Making Butter: Pour a small amount of whipping cream in small containers such as baby food jars. Children shake jars until whipping cream turns to butter. Spread the butter onto crackers and enjoy!

Books: Farm Life

Big Red Barn by Margaret Wise Brown. Scholastic, 1956.

Cock-A-Doodle-Doo by Franz Brandenberg. Greenwillow, 1986.

Farm Counting Book by Jane Miller. Scholastic, 1983.

The Milk Makers by Gail Gibbons. Macmillan, 1985.

Piggybook by Anthony Browne. Knopf, 1986.

See page 91 for Farm Life Certificate.

Week 2: Farm Life

Special Days

Monday: Make a scarecrow by stuffing a man's old shirt and pants with newspaper or straw. Use a pair of pantyhose for the head and stuff it with newspaper. Decorate the face with markers, or you may want to sew on buttons for the eyes and nose. For a finishing touch, dress the scarecrow in an old straw hat, boots, and gloves. Place the scarecrow on a chair as part of Farm Life Week.

Tuesday: The story *Flip and the Cows* can be shared as we dress in brown and black today like horses and cows.

Wednesday: Provide a variety of cheeses for children to taste. You may also want to provide each child with a slice of American cheese and a toothpick. Allow the children to draw on their pieces of cheese with their toothpicks before eating.

Thursday: Prepare for the county fair throughout the week. Children bake cookies, cakes, cupcakes, and tarts. They can also draw pictures for art exhibits at the fair. Encourage children to come up with original ideas for fair exhibits. Display all of the items that children make and hand out blue ribbons to everyone.

Friday: Whip up some omelettes for snacktime (page 85).

Circle Time

1. Introduce the concept of the harvest to Circle Time by showing pictures of different types of harvests from library books or magazines. As you show the pictures, discuss with children what happens during harvest time on a farm. Encourage children to express how they think it would feel to ride a combine, run in a wheat field, and be a part of a harvest.
   Farm Life/ Harvest Time

2. Show children some of the products that come from a farm. You may want to bring in milk, yogurt, ice cream, cheese, vegetables, and eggs. Ask each child to tell which product is his or her favorite.
   Farm Products/Cognitive Skills

3. Give one child a toy farm animal. Tell the child not to show the toy to the rest of the group. The child then describes the animal to the group (without giving away its name) until someone guesses the type of animal. Continue with the game until everyone has had a turn describing an animal. Have fun singing "I'm a Little Piglet" at the end of Circle Time:

I'm a Little Piglet
(Sung to the tune of "I'm a Little Teapot")

I'm a little piglet who loves to play;
In the mud all day I will stay.
My tail is curly, any food I will take;
Oink, oink, oink is the noise I make.

Guessing Game/Communication/Music

4. Cut several colors of award ribbons from colored paper. Design them to look like county fair ribbons. Place them in a container. Have each child choose a ribbon and announce the color of the ribbon. Then, pin the ribbons on the children so they can wear them all day.
County Fair/Color Recognition

Art Activities

Straw Art: Children paint using pieces of straw as their paintbrushes. When paintings are finished, the pieces of straw can be added to the paintings for effect.

Creative Milk Cartons: Give each child a milk carton to decorate. Make available fabric pieces, yarn, buttons, paper scraps, and other collage material for children to glue on their cartons.

My Very Own Horse: Cut out horse shapes from different colors of construction paper. Each child chooses a horse, glues it onto a piece of paper, and then draws him- or herself riding the horse. To add fun and a sense of ownership, have children name their horses.

Tasty Treats

Omelettes: Whip eggs in a large container. Add a small amount of milk and season with salt and pepper. Using an electric skillet, make a small omelette for each child. Sprinkle cheese over eggs while cooking.

Grain in a Trough: Prepare trail mix by mixing together raisins, oat cereal, nuts, cheese crackers, and popcorn. Serve in small boxes that resemble miniature troughs.

Books: Farm Life

Flip by Wesley Dennis. Scholastic, 1973.

Flip and the Cows by Wesley Dennis. Scholastic, 1942.

Rosie's Walk by Pat Hutchins. Macmillan, 1968.

Small Pig by Arnold Lobel. Harper & Row, 1969.

See page 91 for Farm Life Certificate.

Week 3: Teddy Bears

Facts

- The teddy bear's name comes from the nickname for Theodore Roosevelt (Teddy). Theodore Roosevelt was America's 26th president. He served in the Oval Office between 1901 and 1909. Roosevelt was associated with the bear after a cartoon was published depicting him saving the life of a bear cub.

- A teddy bear is a stuffed, cuddly toy animal resembling a bear.

- Teddy bears are the preferred sleeping companions of many children.

Special Days

Monday: Children come to school dressed in brown like bears or with teddy bears on their clothing. Gather in a circle to compare and contrast each child's clothing.

Tuesday: Read aloud the story of *The Three Bears*. After reading the story, choose children to act out the different roles. Use props (such as chairs or boxes) to represent the beds.

Wednesday: Provide a special table on which to display teddy bear books and poems. A favorite bear story is *Corduroy*. Share this book today.

Thursday: Plan a picnic for children and their special guests—teddy bears! Peanut butter and jelly sandwiches, chips, and milk will be the fare for the day. Spread a big checkered tablecloth on the floor upon which bears and children can sit.

Friday: Sip on Root Bear Floats at snacktime (page 87).

Circle Time

1. Bring a teddy bear to Circle Time. Each child tells a story about the bear, which is then copied into a big pad of paper. Throughout the week, children add to the story each day. Provide added enjoyment by having children illustrate the teddy bear book.
   Storytelling/Art

2. Cut bear shapes from different colors of construction paper. Give a different colored bear to each child. Repeat the saying: "Brown bear, brown bear, who do you see?" The child with the brown bear responds: "I see a purple bear looking at me." Children continue this pattern around the circle until all of the children have had a chance to respond.
   Rhythmic Play/Color Recognition

3. Supply a teddy bear and blanket for children to take home for a night. Each day, a different child takes the bear home. The day after each child takes the bear and blanket

home, he or she relates where the bear was taken and answers such questions as "Did you sleep with it?" "Did the bear join you for meals?" etc.
Imaginative Play/Communication

4. Pass a teddy bear around the room. Ask children questions such as "How does holding the teddy bear make you feel?" "Is it hard or soft?" "What special color or other characteristics does the bear have?" Have children recite the following chant and mimic the motions described:

Teddy Bear Jump Up High

Teddy bear, teddy bear, turn around;
Teddy bear, teddy bear, touch the ground.
Teddy bear, teddy bear, bend your knees;
Teddy bear, teddy bear, take a bow please.
Teddy bear, teddy bear, jump up high;
Teddy bear, teddy bear, touch the sky.
Teddy bear, teddy bear, wiggle your nose;
Teddy bear, teddy bear, grab your toes.
Teddy bear, teddy bear, take a seat;
Teddy bear, teddy bear, rest your feet.

Observation/Gross Motor Activity/Following Directions

Art Activities

Teddy Bear's Picnic: Spread a large piece of newsprint on a table. Make available markers and crayons. Children create a teddy bear's picnic on paper.

Dressed-Up Bears: Cut a large teddy bear out of tagboard. Provide children with buttons, yarn, and fabric scraps to glue on the bear's body to represent facial features and clothes. Display the completed bear on a wall.

The Three Bears Puppets: Cut out many bear shapes from brown construction paper. Children glue bears onto popsicle sticks and use crayons and markers to decorate them. They can act out the story of "The Three Bears" with their puppets.

Bear Collage: Place a variety of bear stickers and construction paper on the art table. Children can place the stickers on their papers and add drawings with their markers.

Tasty Treats

Root Bear Floats: Place a scoop of ice cream in each child's glass. Children pour in root beer to make ice cream floats.

Teddy Bear Cookies: Use prepared cookie dough and have children make a teddy bear shape with their portions. This is easily done by rolling small balls of dough for the head, body, legs, and arms. Place the balls together to resemble a teddy bear. Push the balls slightly flat and decorate with raisins. Bake according to the directions on the cookie package.

Three Bears Porridge: Make oatmeal by following package directions. To accompany the oatmeal, children may choose to add brown sugar, milk, or graham crackers.

Books: Teddy Bears

Corduroy by Don Freeman. Scholastic, 1973.

Humphrey's Bear by Jan Wahl. Henry Holt & Co., 1987.

It's About Time, Jesse Bear by Nancy White Carlstrom. Macmillan, 1990.

This Is the Bear by Sarah Hayes. J.B. Lippincott, 1986.

We're Going on a Bear Hunt retold by Michael Rosen. Macmillan, 1989.

See page 92 for Teddy Bears Certificate.

Week 4: Summer Weather

Facts

- In the Northern Hemisphere, the Summer season occurs from the middle of June through the middle of September.

- Summer is the period between the Summer solstice (the longest day of the year) and the autumnal equinox (the time of year in which the Sun crosses the celestial equator and the length of day and night are equal).

- The longest day of the year occurs sometime around June 21.

- In the Northern Hemisphere, Summer is the warmest time of the year as the heat from the Sun is most directly felt during this season.

- Appropriate clothing needs to be worn during the Summer in order to stay as cool as possible.

- Family vacations are usually taken during the Summer since most children are out of school. This is changing somewhat in our society, however, as many schools are operating year-round.

Special Days

Monday: Cut out many large circles from newsprint. Children can then paint the circles yellow like the Sun. When the circles have dried, staple two circles together around the edges and stuff with newsprint. Hang the Sun shapes from the ceiling. You may want to taste Sunshine Balls today (page 90). Also look through *Sun's Up*, a wordless picture book about the Sun's rising.

Tuesday: Children bring swimsuits to school to be worn for the various water activities. Suggested water activities include playing in a sprinkler, a wading pool, a water table and playing with water toys appropriate for the water table.

Wednesday: Children wear their favorite hats or visors to protect them from the Sun. They may want to make their own visors, as well (see page 90 for instructions).

Thursday: Prepare a beach party on your playground. Use sand to create a beach and a blue tarpaulin to represent the ocean. Throw down some beach towels for sun bathing, shovels and pails for digging, and beach balls for bouncing. Children can pretend to jump from the sandy beach into the ocean.

Friday: A cool treat for a hot day is homemade fruit juice popsicles (page 90).

Circle Time

1. Pack a suitcase with Winter and Summer clothing. Pass the suitcase around the group, allowing each child time to pull out appropriate Summer clothing. Ask each child to explain why he or she feels that the chosen article of clothing is best for Summer wear. Follow the Summer clothing discussion with a relaxing poem about Summer heat:

   ### Summer Heat

   In Summer, when the days are hot,
   I try to find a shady spot.
   I hardly move a single bit,
   And sit, and sit, and sit, and sit.

   Summer Clothing/Poetry

2. Draw a beach scene on a large piece of newsprint and secure it to the wall at a height the children can reach. Children add to the beach scene by drawing items they would take with them for a day at the seashore. For a different approach, make available teacher-prepared objects (such as sand pails, shovels, swimsuits, sun screen) for children to glue on the newsprint. As each child chooses an object to be added to the picture, encourage him or her to tell why that particular object was chosen.
   Art/Communication

3. Discuss with the children the many uses of water. Some starter ideas are showers, baths, drinking, swimming, watering plants, and washing clothes.
   Discussion/Water Use

4. Cut out circles of different colors from construction paper. Make a large construction paper cone. Ask children to tell their favorite ice cream flavors. Write each child's name and his or her favorite flavor on the ice cream scoop (circle) and place it on the large cone. Display the ice cream cone on the wall.
Discussion/Cognitive Skills

Art Activities

Sponge Sunshine: Cut sponges into circle shapes and have children dip the sponges into yellow and orange paint to create sunshine on paper.

A Summer Picture: Precut from construction paper clouds, suns, grass, wavy oceans, tents, and anything else that makes you think of Summer weather. Children choose from among the available items to create their own Summer scenes.

Toe Painting: Children take off their shoes and socks for this activity! Children sit on chairs placed in front of a large piece of white paper and dip their toes into paint to create toe paintings.

Water Painting: On a sunny day, give each child a bucket and a paintbrush. Have the children fill their buckets with water and pretend to paint the sidewalk, playground equipment, school building, etc.

Sun Visors: Cut paper plates in half and then cut around the rim of the plates. Use a hole puncher to make holes on both ends of each plate's rim. Add string or yarn to secure visors to the children's heads.

Tasty Treats

Popsicles: Pour fruit juices into ice cube trays or small cups. Cut straws into thirds and stick in popsicles. Freeze until ready to eat.

Strawberries Dipped in Yogurt: Use fresh strawberries with the stems left on. Children dip their strawberries in strawberry yogurt.

Sunshine Balls: Use a melon scooper to make melon balls. You may want to use a cantaloupe to represent the color of sunshine.

Books: Summer Weather

For Sand Castles or Sea Shells by Gail Hartman. Bradbury Press, 1990.

It's Summer by Richard L. Allington and Kathleen Krull. Raintree Children's Books, 1981.

Summer Cat by Howard Knotts. Harper & Row, 1981.

Sun's Up by Teryl Eurremer. Crown Publishers, 1987.

D.W. All Wet by March Brown. Little, Brown & Co., 1988.

See page 92 for Summer Weather Certificate.

FARM LIFE

_____
(child's name)

had a farm

EIEIO!

FARM LIFE

I harvested a bumper crop of lessons about life on the farm.

My name is:_____

Teddy Bears

I hugged a Teddy Bear today!

My name is: _____

Summer Weather

I shine bright as the sun.

My name is: _____

July

Theme	Monday	Tuesday	Wednesday	Thursday	Friday
Fourth of July Celebration	Wear red, white, and blue	Visit a hot dog stand/have a picnic to celebrate U.S.A.'s birthday	American Flag Parade	Patriotic movement	Cooking Day: Flags on Crackers
Ocean Life	Starfish Hunt	Wear blue like the ocean	Shell Sharing Day	Shark Day	Cooking Day: Shark Soup
Ocean Life	Taste sardines and oysters	Sand sculpting	Draw an ocean mural	Fishing Day	Cooking Day: Octopus
Transportation	Trike Wash	Bring in a toy that represents travel	Train Ride Day	Field trip: Visit the airport	Cooking Day: Airline Snack
Extra Days	Extra Day: Wear a shape on your clothing	Extra Day: Wear gray like a shark or whale	Extra Day: Trike Trip		

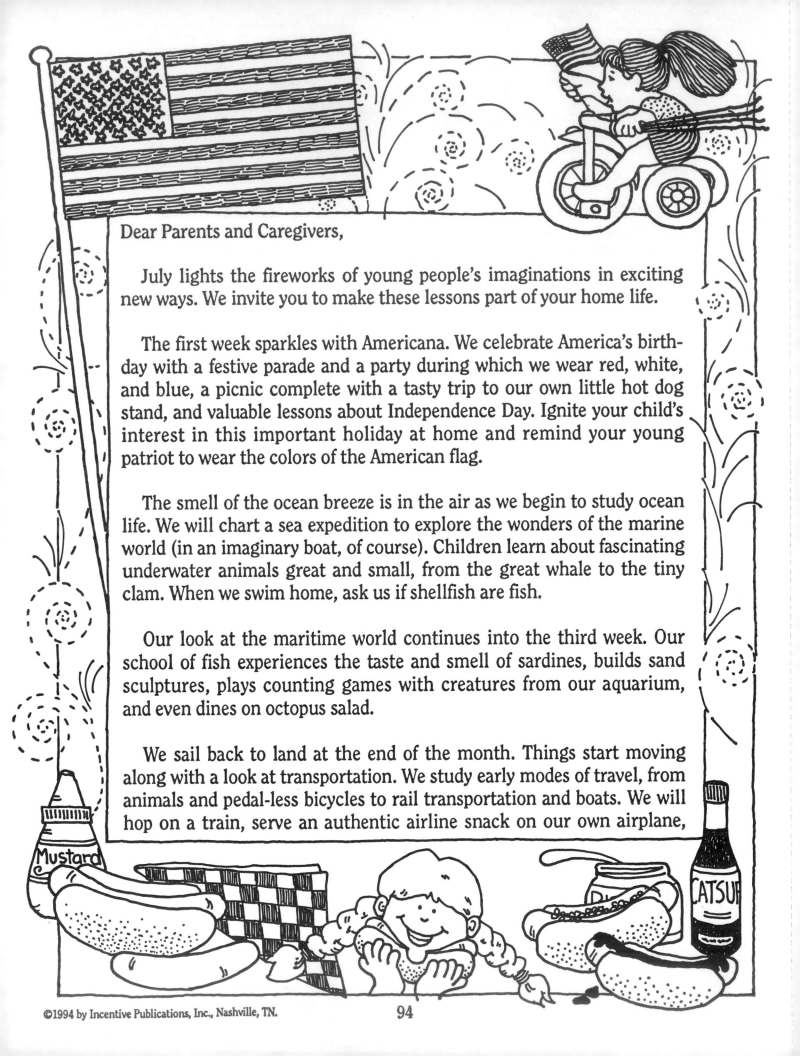

Dear Parents and Caregivers,

July lights the fireworks of young people's imaginations in exciting new ways. We invite you to make these lessons part of your home life.

The first week sparkles with Americana. We celebrate America's birthday with a festive parade and a party during which we wear red, white, and blue, a picnic complete with a tasty trip to our own little hot dog stand, and valuable lessons about Independence Day. Ignite your child's interest in this important holiday at home and remind your young patriot to wear the colors of the American flag.

The smell of the ocean breeze is in the air as we begin to study ocean life. We will chart a sea expedition to explore the wonders of the marine world (in an imaginary boat, of course). Children learn about fascinating underwater animals great and small, from the great whale to the tiny clam. When we swim home, ask us if shellfish are fish.

Our look at the maritime world continues into the third week. Our school of fish experiences the taste and smell of sardines, builds sand sculptures, plays counting games with creatures from our aquarium, and even dines on octopus salad.

We sail back to land at the end of the month. Things start moving along with a look at transportation. We study early modes of travel, from animals and pedal-less bicycles to rail transportation and boats. We will hop on a train, serve an authentic airline snack on our own airplane, and make license plates for our bikes—and to eat! We will learn about the Wright brothers and the first man-carrying airplane. We take our lessons above and beyond when we consider the importance of the space shuttle.

Sincerely yours,

_____

Octopus: A Taste of Ocean Life

A hot dog becomes an octopus when you make a lengthwise slice halfway down the hot dog and cut the two slices lengthwise again. This makes arms for your octopus. Place hot dog in boiling water and watch the arms curl up. Remove from water and serve with ketchup or mustard.

Ocean Life Fingerplay: Five Little Fish

One fish swimming through the blue—
Another showed up; then there were two.
Two fish wiggling by me—
Another joined them; then there were three.
Three fish knocking at the door—
Another joined them; then there were four.
Four fish went for a dive—
Another joined them; then there were five.
Five fish playing in the sea—
They swam around, free as can be.

Week 1: Fourth Of July Celebration

Facts

- Every year on the fourth of July, the United States celebrates the anniversary of the adoption of the Declaration of Independence.

- The Declaration of Independence was written by Thomas Jefferson and signed by the Second Continental Congress on July 4, 1776. This formal statement declared the thirteen colonies free and independent of Great Britain.

- Traditional ways of celebrating this special day include flying the American flag, picnics, band concerts, parades, and fireworks displays.

Special Days

Monday: Create a festive environment at school today. Decorate hallways and classrooms with red, white, and blue streamers. Encourage children to wear these colors to school.

Tuesday: Build a hot dog stand out of a cardboard box and have children paint and decorate the box. Hold a picnic, during which children take turns distributing hot dogs and buns from the stand.

Wednesday: Give a small American flag to each child to carry in your Fourth of July parade. Provide a variety of musical instruments for children to play (some suggestions are bells, cymbals, and triangles). Have some children ride tricycles and some walk in the parade.

Thursday: Connect red, white, and blue streamers to a toilet paper roll or a stick. Play patriotic music and have children move their streamers to the beat. Ask children to wave their streamers, high, low, side to side, fast, slow, etc.

Friday: Enjoy a patriotic snack of Flags on Crackers (page 97).

Circle Time

1. Make a folder game with several different sizes of stars. Cut two stars of each size, using the colors red, white, and blue. Glue one set of stars on the folder and laminate it. Laminate the other set of stars for children to match with the stars in the folder. *Matching/Sizes and Colors*

2. Cut out strips of paper using red, white, and blue construction paper. Give each child a set of the colored strips. Ask each child to pick up a strip of a specified color and place it in a certain location ("behind you, on your head, on your shoulders," etc.). *Color Recognition/Following Directions*

3. Make a large flag from construction paper; cut out the stars separately. Each day, have

a different child count out a specified number of stars and place them on the flag. By the end of the week, there should be 50 stars on the flag (one for each state!).
Math/Counting

4. Begin Circle Time by reciting the poem "Independence Day." Bring a picnic basket to the group and pretend that you are hosting an Independence Day picnic. Ask children what they would bring along with them to a picnic. Supply magazines for the children and have them cut or tear out pictures of items they would like to bring to a picnic. Have all children name their objects and place them in the picnic basket.

Independence Day

Lights light up the dark, black sky.
Fireworks burst way up high.
Loud sounds surprised our ears;
Picnics have been celebrated on this day for years.
What holiday is this?

Imaginative Play/Poem

Art Activities

Tissue Paper Flag: Draw lines on white construction paper to resemble the stripes of the American flag. Cut small squares of red, white, and blue tissue paper. Children dip squares of tissue paper in liquid starch and place them on the construction paper flag.

Fireworks: Show children pictures of evening fireworks and then have children draw their own pictures of a fireworks display on dark blue paper. Visit children individually and have each one tell you about his or her picture. Write their stories in a notebook and read them aloud at a later time.

Sky Fireworks: Children cut black construction paper into circles to fit in pie pans. Drop a variety of colored paint and a marble in each pan and have children paint a nighttime fireworks scene.

Glitter Painting: Mix glitter with glue. Using a brush, children spread the glittery glue on pieces of black construction paper. A pipe cleaner can be glued to the paper to resemble a sparkler.

Tasty Treats

Flags on Crackers: Make frosting by mixing a small amount of milk with powdered sugar; stir until the mixture has thickened to spreading consistency. Divide frosting into three equal parts and color two of the sections with red and blue food coloring, leaving the third part white. Spread on saltine crackers.

Red, White, and Blue Snack: Children spoon strawberries and blueberries into their bowls and top with whipped cream.

Books: Fourth of July Celebration

Fourth of July by Barbara M. Joosse. Alfred A. Knopf, 1985.

Henry's Fourth of July by Holly Keller. Greenwillow Books, 1985.

See page 105 for Fourth of July Celebration Certificate.

Week 2: Ocean Life

Facts

- Whales, the largest animals in the world, are mammals which live in the sea. Whale babies are born alive and are nursed by their mothers. A baby blue whale has been recorded as weighing as much as four tons.

- The sperm whale is the only whale with teeth; its teeth are located on its lower jaw only. Other types of whales do not have any teeth. Instead, they have enormous strainers which somewhat resemble human fingernails. These strainers are useful because the whale swims through the ocean with its mouth open wide, letting in shrimp and other small sea creatures. When the whale closes its mouth, the water inside is forced out, but the food supply is contained in the whale's strainers.

- Shellfish, such as clams and oysters, are not fish. Their proper name is mollusk. Mollusks have soft bodies protected in mantles. In most cases, mollusks manufacture or secrete their own hard shells.

- Fish breathe through gills, organs which are located behind a fish's head. There is one gill on each side of a fish's head. Gills function in much the same way as human lungs.

- The great white shark is the most dangerous of the shark species. This shark has a large jaw and sharp teeth. The great white shark lives and swims in mostly warm and temperate water, but will occasionally enter colder water. This shark has been known to attack man. Other sharks that have attacked people are the hammerhead and tiger sharks. These fish are attracted to prey by the scent of blood and water vibrations.

- The ocean's water level rises and falls twice a day. Tides are caused by the gravitational force of the Moon and the Sun on the water.

Special Days

Monday: Cut starfish shapes out of tagboard and hide them in a sandy area. Have children dig in the sand to find the starfish.

Tuesday: Create an ocean atmosphere by hanging strips of blue cellophane paper from the ceiling. Encourage children to wear the color blue on their clothing.

Wednesday: Large, medium, and small seashells appear at school today. Provide a special table on which shells are placed for children to touch, smell, and listen for ocean sounds.

Thursday: Hang a stuffed shark from the ceiling to add to the ocean atmosphere. Here's how to make one: double newsprint before cutting the outline of a shark. Staple the edges together, and leave an opening to stuff with newspaper. Make a maze on the floor using masking tape and have children pretend to be sharks in the ocean following the maze. Hang pictures of sharks on the classroom walls for children to observe.

Friday: Serve Shark Soup to celebrate Ocean Life Week (page 100).

Circle Time

1. Take an imaginary trip to the sea. Climb in your yacht, put on life preservers, start the motor, and begin your journey to observe ocean life. Allow each child to share the sea life that he or she sees on the journey.
   Imaginative Play/Ocean Life

2. Spread blue butcher paper on the length of a table, or use newsprint that has been colored blue. Precut seaweed, starfish, shark, whale, clam, and other sea life shapes out of colored paper. Children choose the sea life that they want to glue on the paper and tell stories of their choice. For a variation on this activity, let children draw the sea life directly on the paper.
   Art/Storytelling

3. Children feel and discuss the differences between wet and dry sand. Place sand in the bottom of a large, clear bowl and fill with water. Place shells, rocks, rubber fish, and anything else found in the ocean in the bowl. Have children put their hands in the bowl and feel the sand and other objects. Discuss with them how the objects feel. You may also want to have them guess which objects they touch.
   Science/Ocean Life

4. Bring fossils of shells to Circle Time and let children examine them. Then, give each child a handful of clay and set out a tray with a variety of shells. Children can create their own fossils by pressing the shells into the clay to make an imprint.
   Science/Making Fossils

Art Activities

Ocean Life: Using crayons, children draw fish on a large piece of newsprint. When they have finished, have children blow watered-down tempera paint onto the paper with straws. This gives the look of water.

Goldfish: Precut small fish out of yellow and orange construction paper. Children then glue the fish on blue construction paper and add their own ideas to the picture using colored markers.

Starfish: Cut out many starfish shapes from tagboard. Children use a brush to spread glue over the starfish. Birdseed is then sprinkled onto the shapes. When the shapes have dried, have children shake off the excess birdseed. This will create the rough look of a starfish.

My Pet Fish: Collect clear plastic drinking cups, sand, and small shells. Cut small fish shapes out of sponges. Each child pours a small amount of sand into a cup, adds a few shells, and fills with water. Each child then chooses a fish and places it in its new home.

Tasty Treats

Shark Soup: Buy shark pasta that comes in a can with sauce. Add carrots, potatoes, tomatoes, celery, and any other soup ingredients to make Shark Soup. Heat to desired temperature.

Tuna Salad: Mix canned tuna with celery, minced onions, pickle relish, and mayonnaise. Serve on bread or on a lettuce leaf.

Books: Ocean Life

A House for Hermit Crab by Eric Carle. Picture Book Studio, 1987.

Just Grandma and Me by Mercer Mayer. Western Publishing Co., 1983.

On My Beach There Are Many Pebbles by Leo Lionni. Obolensky, 1961.

Sand Cake by Frank Asch. Parents' Magazine Press, 1978.

See page 105 for Ocean Life Certificate.

Week 3: Ocean Life

Special Days

Monday: Provide canned sardines and oysters for children to taste and smell. Write down how each child reacted to the sardines and oysters and read their statements aloud during Circle Time.

Tuesday: Wet a section of the sand area to allow children to create sand sculptures. Make available sand molds, shovels, and pails.

Wednesday: Spread a long sheet of blue paper on a sidewalk. Pour yellow and orange paint in flat containers and place by the edge of the paper. Children dip their feet in the paint and walk across the paper. When their footprints have dried, have children use markers to create fish from their footprints. Display the fish mural for all to view during Ocean Life Week.

Thursday: Make fishing poles for children out of dowel rods and string. Fish can be made from tagboard. Be sure to punch a hole on one end of the fish. Turn a card table on its side and cover the top with blue paper to represent the ocean. Fishers cast their lines over the top of the card table where the teacher, or an older child, ties fish to their lines. Repeat this activity until each child has had a chance to cast a line.

Friday: Eat an octopus for snack today (page 102).

Circle Time

1. Gather ocean life artifacts from the beach or purchase them from a store. Share these treasures during Circle Time. Suggested items include starfish, various shells, seaweed, coral, and sand dollars. Children delight in touching and smelling artifacts from the sea shore, as well as listening to the ocean sounds heard in some shells.
   Science/Ocean Life

2. Design an aquarium out of blue tagboard. Draw ferns and shells in it for a realistic look. Cut ten or more fish from orange, gray, and yellow paper. (Your game will last longer if you laminate both the fish and the aquarium.) To play, children count a specified number of fish and place them in the aquarium. For a variation, put sticky dots on index cards, and place a card with a certain number of dots above the aquarium. Children count that number of fish and place them in the aquarium.
   Math/Counting

3. Draw and color a pair of eyes on the top of each child's hand. Explain to the group that their hands are now crabs. The crabs can crawl around on the floor and up the walls. Ask each child what he or she thinks it would feel like to be a crab.
   Imaginative Play/Communication

4. Make a variety of fish of different colors and sizes for the flannelboard. Each child takes turns choosing a fish and describing it to the others. Make sure everyone puts their fish back in the water (on the flannelboard). After all children have had a turn, ask each to recall which fish he or she picked.
   Description/Memory

Art Activities

Seaweed Collage: Collect seaweed from the beach and ask children to design a collage made of seaweed on precut pieces of tagboard. If seaweed is unavailable, cut seaweed shapes from colored paper. Make a frame border in which to place the collages. You can vary this project by using small shells instead of seaweed.

Octopus: Give each child a toilet paper roll and scissors. Children cut nine lines halfway up the roll. These slits will form the octopus's legs. Bend up the legs, decorate with markers, and you'll have an octopus with eight legs.

Paper Plate Fish: Trace a triangle on the outer edge of a paper plate. (The triangle's point should be pointing to the middle of the plate.) Supply one plate to each child who will then cut out the triangle and staple it to the opposite side of the plate. The cut-out portion of the plate resembles the mouth, and the triangle forms the tail of a fish. Each child can decorate his or her paper fish with markers or crayons.

Tasty Treats

Octopus: A hot dog becomes an octopus when you make a lengthwise slice halfway down the hot dog and cut the two slices lengthwise again. This makes arms for your octopus. Place hot dog in boiling water and watch the arms curl up. Remove from water and serve with ketchup or mustard.

Jelly Fish: Cut a fish shape from a piece of bread using a cookie cutter or a knife. Toast the bread and spread with your favorite jelly.

Fish Pizzas: Cut a triangle out of one half of an english muffin, and place it on the opposite half (similar to Paper Plate Fish above). Sprinkle muffin with shredded cheese and melt in a microwave or conventional oven.

Books: Ocean Life

Dinosaur Beach by Liza Donnelly. Scholastic, 1989.

How To Hide an Octopus and Other Sea Creatures by Ruth Heller. Grosset & Dunlap, 1985.

Sand Castle by Ronald Wegen. Greenwillow Books, 1977.

Sand Dollar, Sand Dollar by Joyce Audy Dos Santos. Lippincott, 1980.

Swimmy by Leo Lionni. Scholastic, 1963.

See page 106 for Ocean Life Certificate.

Week 4: Transportation

Facts

- An early mode of transportation was the bicycle. The bicycle was cheaper than traveling by horse and buggy. The first bicycle was designed without pedals; the rider moved the bicycle by pushing on the ground with his or her feet.

- Steam-powered railroad transportation was developed during the 1830s. One of the most elegant passenger trains was the Orient Express, a luxury train which traveled across Europe. The longest railroad in the world runs across lands in the former Soviet Union. The Amtrak railway line has become more widely used in the United States during the last few decades; however, as other modes of transportation have been developed, the popularity of train travel has declined.

- The Wright Brothers produced the first man-carrying airplane. Their invention drastically altered how humans think of travel. Before passenger airplanes were invented, travel by foot, horses, buses, cars, or trains took a great deal of time. Airplanes, however, can reduce a trip that might take days or weeks into one that takes only a few hours. Most passenger planes are actually jets, which fly at a cruising altitude of about 30,000 feet.

- Until the 18th century, humans used animals as a source of transportation. In many parts of the world, people still use horses, camels, elephants, dog teams, or donkeys as a means of traveling.

- Some other modes of transportation are hot air balloons, gliders, kayaks, rafts, canoes, submarines, vans, buses, and recreational vehicles.

- The space shuttle is a vehicle that transports humans into space. The shuttle takes off from the Earth carrying astronauts and a workload (a group of experiments). Once in space the astronauts perform experiments and gather information about our planet and solar system. The shuttle is equipped to stay in space for weeks at a time.

Special Days

Monday: Tricycles are washed with pails of soapy water and scrub brushes. Children will have fun using water hoses to squirt their tricycles—and each other!

Tuesday: Toy cars, trucks, buses, airplanes, ambulances, helicopters, fire engines, and boats are just a few of the modes of transportation brought to school today.

Wednesday: Use various sizes of boxes to make a train for the playground.

Thursday: Make prior arrangements to take a tour of your local airport. If there is no airport in your area, visit a local bus or train depot.

Friday: Have an airline snack today (page 104).

Circle Time

1. Describe to the children the many ways there are to travel. Ask each child how he or she would prefer to travel when on vacation. Suggest wild and crazy ideas for the children to consider, such as riding on camels, elephants, rickshaws, and feet! Write down each child's preferred mode of transportation and place in a scrapbook to be read throughout the week.
   Transportation/Imaginative Thought

2. Draw a picture of a wheel on a large piece of newsprint. During Circle Time, discuss wheeled vehicles. How many different types of wheeled vehicles have the children ridden in? Their answers may include carriages, strollers, bicycles, cars, stagecoaches, trains, and buses. Keep the wheel on the wall for the entire week. As each day passes, the children will think of more wheeled vehicles.
Wheeled Vehicles/Generating Thought

3. Make a train, boat, car, airplane, bus, and bicycle for the flannelboard. Ask children which vehicle has wings, two tires, a caboose, rides on water, moves on tracks, etc.
Transportation/Categorizing

4. Make a bus from newsprint and hang it on a wall near the place you gather for Circle Time. Sing "The Wheels on the Bus" and have children add the words "kids," "baby," "dog," "wheel," "daddy," "mother," etc., as you sing the song.
Transportation/Song

Art Activities

Tire Prints: Roll toy cars through black paint and across a sheet of white paper.

Boats: Cut corkboard into a small rectangle to make the base of a boat (one for each child). Then have each child glue a precut triangle onto a toothpick and stick in the boat's base. Boats can be floated in a water table or a child's pool filled with water.

License Plates: Cut rectangles from tagboard to resemble license plates. Children glue precut letters and numbers on their license plates. When they ride their tricycles, children can tape the plates on the backs of the trikes.

Tasty Treats

Airline Snacks: During snacktime, line up chairs to simulate an airplane's cabin and serve small packages of nuts and cups of juice.

License Plates: Graham crackers are cut in half to resemble the shape of a license plate. Children spread peanut butter on their crackers and add alphabet cereal to create a license plate's numbers and letters.

Books: Transportation

Bears on Wheels by Stan and Jan Berenstain. Random House, 1969.

Freight Train by Donald Crews. Greenwillow Books, 1978.

School Bus by Donald Crews. Scholastic, 1984.

Truck by Donald Crews. Greenwillow Books, 1980.

Wheels by Venice Shone. Scholastic, 1990.

See page 106 for Transportation Certificate.

Fourth of July Celebration

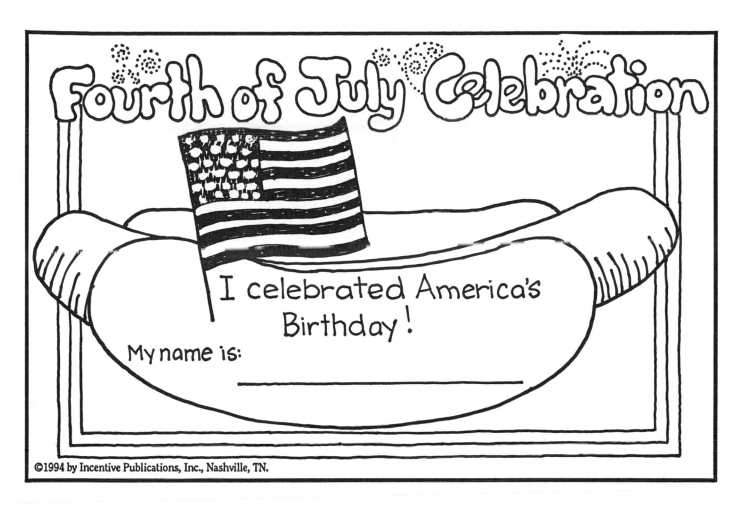

I celebrated America's Birthday!

My name is:

_____

OCEAN LIFE

My name is: _____

I charted a learning expedition to the beautiful sea.

I learned more about the sea and had some ocean adventures.

My name is: _____

ocean life

TRANSPORTATION

LEARNER'S PERMIT

FOR
TRANSPORTATION STUDY

Presented to

_____

(child's name)

August

Theme	Monday	Tuesday	Wednesday	Thursday	Friday
Camping	Bring in a canteen	Roast a marshmallow	Pitch a tent for Camp-Out Day	Make backpacks and take a hike	Cooking Day: S'mores
Ecology	Mother Earth visit	Litter Walk	Tree celebration	Wear green like grass and trees	Cooking Day: Trees
Nighttime	Bring in your favorite bedtime story	Star gazing	Wear your pajamas to school	Read *There's a Nightmare in My Closet*/share nighttime fears	Cooking Day: Milk and cookies
Vacations	Make and mail postcards	Wear a vacation shirt	Share a souvenir from a vacation	Bring a vacation picture to school	Cooking Day: Fast food meal
Extra Days	Extra Day: Share a new word you have learned	Extra Day: Sidewalk chalk writing	Extra Day: Bring in an item that can be recycled		

Dear Parents and Caregivers,

The upcoming Summer days are anything but lazy. At school, August hums with many different kinds of learning experiences.

The first week makes happy campers out of all of us. We learn how to go camping, from pitching a tent and cooking over a campfire to making a backpack and binoculars and appreciating the special rules of the great outdoors. If you can, plan a camping trip or camp out in your backyard.

Our world is very important, and we will learn ways to take care of it during Ecology Week. Mother Earth will pay a visit and share ways that we can help the Earth. We will take a litter walk, celebrate trees, and even eat miniature trees. Ask your child what we've learned about water and energy conservation and reducing garbage, air pollution, and hazardous household waste. Practice Earth-friendly habits around the house to reinforce these lessons and make them a part of your life.

During our week of nighttime fun, we will learn about the phases of the Moon and appreciate the beauty of stars. Remind your small dreamer to bring pajamas for our pajama party! We will share favorite bedtime stories and gently discuss some of our nighttime fears. This would be a good time to discuss them at home, also.

During Vacation Week we will take a break from work and head out for an imaginary holiday. Our dream vacation is complete—we pack a

DO NOT Litter

I ♥ Trash!

suitcase, load up the car for our journey, play inventive car games, string cereal on a necklace for a handy road snack, and send handmade postcards to the folks back home. Be sure your child brings in a photograph from a trip.

So come along for the ride, and bring the important lessons of August home to your family. We look forward to sharing the trip with you.

Sincerely yours,

_____

A Tasty Treat for Camping: S'Mores

Stack a fourth of a chocolate bar and a marshmallow on top of a graham cracker. Top with another graham cracker. Wrap in aluminum foil and place in the sun to melt.

Vacation Fingerplay: Ten Little Postcards

1 little, 2 little, 3 little postcards,
4 little, 5 little, 6 little postcards,
7 little, 8 little, 9 little postcards,
10 little postcards dropped in the mail.

Week 1: Camping

Facts

- Camping is a popular way to spend a weekend or holiday in America.
- There are many different ways to camp. Some choose to camp in recreational vehicles or cabins that have all of the comforts of home. Others enjoy "roughing it" by camping in tents with sleeping bags.

Special Days

Monday: Children fill their canteens with water supplied by the teacher. Take an imaginary trip to the desert where there is no water available. Pretend that the weather is so hot and dry that you must quench your thirst with water from the canteen.

Tuesday: Gather sticks and build an imaginary campfire. Each child should receive a stick and a marshmallow to roast over the campfire.

Wednesday: The teacher or a parent can provide the tent needed today. Assemble the tent inside the classroom or outdoors. A pretend game of tug-of-war is fun to play during your imaginary camp-out. Separate the group into two teams and have them pull on an imaginary rope.

Thursday: Children make their own backpacks today (see page 111 for instructions). Arrange to take a hike (backpacks included!) to look for squirrels, birds, bears, and other forest creatures. The story *Blaze a Trail* will be fun to read today.

Friday: Warm S'mores outdoors and eat them at snacktime (page 111).

Circle Time

1. Hold Circle Time under a blanket propped up by chairs. Pretend the group is camping in a tent. Ask children to imagine where the tent is pitched. Is it by the ocean? in the mountains? by a bubbling brook? etc. Also ask the group to decide what they want to cook for dinner, if they hear noises outside the tent, if there are bears nearby, etc.
   Camping/Imaginative Play

2. Bring to class a packed backpack. Pull out of the backpack items that are needed for a camping trip. Ask each child to choose items to pack for a camping adventure.
   Camping/Creative Thinking

3. Have children imagine that they are going on a camping trip. Ask them questions about their trips: "What will you bring to sleep in?" "What kinds of clothes will you wear?" "What will you eat and how will you cook?" "How will you get there?" etc.
   Camping/Creative Thinking

4. Bring a pair of binoculars to Circle Time. Let each child take a turn looking through the binoculars and describing an object. The other children try to guess the item being described.
   Communication/Guessing Game

5. Pile several sticks together and make a "campfire" by placing red and yellow strips of construction paper on sticks. During Circle Time, sit around the "campfire," and take turns telling stories of camping trips. Share the following fingerplay:

Three Marshmallows

I'm roasting three marshmallows on my stick.
One's for my mommy; she likes hers ooey.
One's for my daddy; he likes his gooey.
One's for me; I like mine chewy.

Storytelling/Fingerplay

Art Activities

Camping Sculpture: Provide items found on a nature walk (pine cones, pine needles, nuts, leaves, etc.). Children stick these items in clay to make a sculpture.

Backpacks: Fold the top of a plain paper bag down several times. Use long strips of construction paper to make the backpack's straps. At the edge of the bag, staple one construction paper strip to the top and the bottom of the sack. Repeat on the other edge of the bag so that you have two straps for the arms. Children may want to decorate their backpacks with crayons or markers.

Binoculars: Tape two toilet paper rolls side-by-side using masking tape. Punch two holes at the top of each roll and string a piece of yarn through the holes. Tie the yarn around the child's neck.

Tasty Treats

Beef Jerky: Purchase beef jerky to be placed in backpacks and eaten on a hike.

S'mores: Stack a fourth of a chocolate bar and a marshmallow on top of a graham cracker. Top with another graham cracker. Wrap in aluminum foil and place in the sun to melt.

Camping Packets of Potatoes and Carrots: Dice potatoes and slice carrots. Place a small amount of each on a square of aluminum foil. Top with a dab of butter or margarine and wrap. Bake in a conventional oven at 350 degrees for 30–40 minutes until potatoes are tender. Supply a packet for each child.

Books: Camping

Author Goes to Camp by Marc Brown. Little, Brown, & Co., 1982.

Blaze a Trail by Stan and Jan Berenstain. Random House, 1987.

Curious George Goes Hiking by Margaret and H.A. Rey and Allan J. Shalleck. Houghton Mifflin, 1985.

Sleep Out by Carol Carrick. Seabury Press, 1973.

The Ten Alarm Camp-Out by Cathy Warren. Lothrop, Lee & Shepard Books, 1983.

See page 119 for Camping Certificate.

Week 2: Ecology

Facts

- The first Earth Day celebration was held on April 22, 1970. An urgent plea for environmental awareness was issued to the world.

- Educators, parents, and communities can help ensure that children learn to protect and care for our environment.

- Individuals can make a difference in the fight to protect the environment. We can make our world a better place to live by actively participating in water conservation, energy conservation, garbage reduction, air pollution reduction, and hazardous household waste reduction.

Special Days

Monday: Find out if there is a Mother Earth in your area. If so, make arrangements for her to visit your class to speak on ecology and conservation. If not, have someone dress up as Mother Earth and offer ways we can become more Earth-friendly.

Tuesday: Take children on a litter walk around the school grounds to spot litter. Make a list of the items you see. Make "trash" collages (see page 113 for instructions).

Wednesday: Contact a local nursery and ask if they would donate a tree to plant at your school. If so, have children participate in planting and taking care of the tree. If there is a tree in your school yard that is good for climbing, allow children to safely climb the tree. You can also play a circle game around a tree. Stroll, skip, hop, clap, and run around the tree.

Thursday: Wear the color green on your clothing, in your hair, and on your clips, bracelets, etc., to celebrate the trees. The book *A Tree Is Nice* would be great to read under the shade of a large tree.

Friday: Munch on Trees today (page 113).

Circle Time

1. Bring recyclable materials such as glass, aluminum, and paper to Circle Time. Have children sort the materials into three separate containers for recycling. Show children a reusable canvas bag and tell them that it is a good alternative to using a plastic or paper bag at the grocery store.
   Recycling/Sorting

2. Attach blue butcher paper to a wall. Make sure that it hangs at the children's eye level. Ask children to pretend that it is a large lake. Have them write their names on precut fish shapes and glue them to the lake. Provide small amounts of trash for children to glue onto the lake as well. Ask children what they think will happen to their fish with all of the litter in the lake. Write their comments on the lake for all to read through-

out the week. Introduce the following poem:

Mother Earth

Where is Mother Earth? Where is Mother Earth?
Here she is. Here she is.
Take care of her water and her land,
For this is where we live and stand.

Environmental Study/Collage/Poetry

3. Collect items such as pencils, barrettes, socks, a cup, a spoon, and some crayons. Also collect pieces of unused trash such as wrappers, crumpled paper, paper towels, tissues, empty cartons, and a small trash can. Place all of the items in front of children; have each child choose one and decide if it should go in the trash can or be reused.

Environmental Study/Conservation

4. Bring to Circle Time a large clear bowl filled with water. Discuss with children the fact that some people litter in our oceans, lakes, and streams and that this hurts the fish and other wildlife living in the water. As you are talking, throw wrappers and trash in the bowl and pour some soda pop in the water. Ask children to discuss their ideas and feelings on this matter.

Water Pollution/Communication

Art Activities

Litter Bags: Provide small brown bags for children to decorate. (Supply pictures of trees for children to paste on their bags.) These bags can be used to collect trash in the car.

Trash Collage: Provide children with art supplies and instruct them to make collages representative of the trash seen on the litter walk.

Creative Drawing: Ask children to imagine how the world would look if everyone took care of it. Then, have them draw a picture of what they imagined. On the backs of their drawings, ask children to create a picture of how the world would look if no one took care of the Earth.

Tasty Treats

Applesauce from a Glass Container: Serve applesauce purchased in a glass container. Discuss the importance of buying foods in recyclable containers. You can top the applesauce with raisins.

Trees: Cut broccoli stalks and top with your favorite salad dressing.

Oscar Trash Cones: Scoop mint chocolate chip ice cream into a cone. Use raisins to decorate the cone with Oscar the Grouch's face.

Books: Ecology

The Giving Tree by Shel Silverstein. Harper & Row, 1964.

The Great Trash Bash by Loreen Leedy. Holiday House, 1991.

AUGUST

The Little Park by Dale Fife. A. Whitman, 1973.

The Tree by Naomi Russell. E.P. Dutton, 1989.

A Tree Is Nice by Janice May Udry. Harper & Row, 1956.

See page 119 for Ecology Certificate.

Week 3: Nighttime

Facts

- Nighttime is the period between the setting of the Sun in the evening and the rising of the Sun in the morning. It is dark during the night.

- The phases of the Moon are determined by the positions of the Moon, the Earth, and the Sun. As the Moon rotates around the Earth, different parts of it are lit by the Sun and visible to the human eye. The first phase is the New Moon Phase, when none of the Moon is visible from the Earth. The Moon appears to increases in size to the Crescent Phase, the popular "slice" of Moon featured in many works of art. The Moon continues to appear to increase in size during the First Quarter Phase and the Gibbous Phase until it reaches the Full Moon Phase. From this point, we watch the Moon appear to decrease in size through the Gibbous, Third Quarter, and Crescent phases until it once again reaches the New Moon Phase. When the Moon appears to be increasing in size, it is called waxing. When the Moon appears to be decreasing in size, it is called waning.

- Preschool children often have fears at night. Many children begin to have nightmares during this stage of their development.

Special Days

Monday: Set up sleeping mats and pillows. This provides a place for children to read their bedtime stories.

Tuesday: Glue glitter on precut stars and decorate your classroom with star constellations hanging from the ceiling. Children can lie on the floor and gaze at the stars. As children look at the stars, recite the following poem:

Starlight

Starlight, star bright,
First star I see tonight.
I wish I may, I wish I might
Get the wish I wish tonight.

114

Wednesday: This is a fun-filled day as children and teacher model different styles of pajamas. A good story to share is *The Beast in the Bathtub.* Point out the cowboy pajamas in the story.

Thursday: Read Mercer Mayer's *There's a Nightmare in My Closet.* This is a good book for prompting children to discuss some of their nighttime fears.

Friday: Relax before naptime with some cookies and milk (page 116).

Circle Time

1. Construct a "What We Do Before Bedtime" poster on a piece of tagboard. Discuss with children what they do before going to bed and have them draw pictures of something they do on the poster. Some ideas are reading a story, taking a bath, brushing teeth, going to the bathroom, saying prayers, and turning on a nightlight.
   Art/Communication

2. Cut several large stars out of tagboard and glue aluminum foil on one side of each of the stars. Tape the stars on a wall near your Circle Time area. Make sure the stars are at a child's eye level. Have each child choose a star and make a wish. Help them write their wishes on the backs of their stars.
   Communication/Writing

3. Ask each child to bring a blanket to Circle Time. Children lie beneath their blankets and pretend to go to sleep. Turn out an imaginary light and read a special nighttime story. You may first want to recite the following poem while acting out the appropriate motions:

   ### Turn Off the Light

   I turn off the lights and jump in my bed.
   I pull the sheets up over my head, and
   I wait for my bedtime story to be read.

   Poem/Creative Play

4. Cut shapes that represent the phases of the Moon from white felt. Place the Moon's phases on the flannelboard and discuss with children how to observe the Moon in the night sky. Use the terms "crescent," "gibbous,"" waxing," and "waning." Children delight in new words and can use these words when observing the Moon's phases.
   Moon's Phases/Vocabulary

Art Activities

Chalk Drawing: Children use colored chalk to draw on pieces of black construction paper.

Shooting Stars: Use a marble to spread colored paint on black construction paper. Use yellow paint to represent shooting stars.

Sunset: Cut out large squares from blue tagboard. Add food coloring to small bottles of glue and mix until the glue is colored. Children squeeze colored glue onto tagboard squares to create sunsets.

Tasty Treats

Milk and Chocolate Chip Cookies:

- 1 cup softened butter or margarine
- ¾ cup brown sugar, packed firmly
- ¾ cup granulated sugar
- 1 teaspoon vanilla
- ½ teaspoon water
- 2 eggs
- 2 cups all-purpose flour
- 1 teaspoon baking soda
- 1 teaspoon salt
- 1 cup chopped nuts (pecans or walnuts)
- 1 package chocolate chips

Beat butter, sugar, vanilla, water, and eggs until light and fluffy. Mix flour with soda and salt; blend into butter mixture. Stir in nuts and chocolate chips. Drop 2 inches apart onto a greased baking sheet. Bake at 375 degrees for 8 to 10 minutes or until golden brown. (Yield: Approx. 8 dozen cookies.) Serve with milk.

Hot Chocolate: Heat milk until warm. Add chocolate syrup to the milk and top with miniature marshmallows.

Popcorn: Pop popcorn for a nighttime snack.

Books: Nighttime

The Beast in the Bathtub by Kathleen Stevens. Harper & Row, 1978.

Franklin in the Dark by Paulete Bourgeois. Scholastic, 1986.

Grandfather Twilight by Barbara Berger. Philomel Books, 1984.

Moongame by Frank Asch. Prentice-Hall, 1984.

There's a Nightmare in My Closet by Mercer Mayer. Dial Books, 1968.

See page 120 for Nighttime Certificate.

Week 4: Vacations

Facts

- Many families take vacations together. Family vacations are usually taken once a year during the summer months when children are out of school.

- Most vacations serve as a time of rest and an escape from the pressures of work and daily routines.

- When on vacation, many people purchase souvenirs and send postcards to friends and relatives.

Special Days

Monday: Purchase blank postcards from the post office and have children color them. After the cards have been colored, the children can share stories about the pictures they have drawn. Assist children in addressing postcards to their parents. Cards may be hand-delivered to parents by the children, or you can walk with them to a mailbox and assist children in mailing them.

Tuesday: Encourage children to wear a shirt or other article of clothing from a previous vacation. Share vacation clothes during Circle Time.

Wednesday: Display vacation souvenirs on a special shelf or table. Children can look at, touch, and smell the souvenirs.

Thursday: Children bring in photographs from previous vacations. Throughout the day, children pin vacation photos on a large bulletin board or cork board for all to enjoy.

Friday: On this vacation day, "drive" to a pretend fast food restaurant for a fun-filled meal (page 118).

Circle Time

1. Begin Circle Time with the fingerplay "Ten Postcards." Display postcards received from places all over the world. Ask each child to choose a postcard and tell a story about the picture. Make a vacation book with each child's story written beneath his or her postcard.

Ten Postcards

1 little, 2 little, 3 little postcards,
4 little, 5 little, 6 little postcards,
7 little, 8 little, 9 little postcards,
10 little postcards dropped in the mail.

Fingerplay/Storytelling

2. Pretend to pack a car in preparation for a vacation. Ask children which items they would take with them on a long car trip, what it would be like to be a car ready to take a long journey, and what the world looks like from a car's perspective.
Travel/Imaginative Play

3. Bring a suitcase and ten articles of clothing to Circle Time. Number index cards from 1 to 10. Each child chooses a card, names that number, and places that many pieces of clothing into the suitcase. Continue until everyone has had a turn.
Math/Counting

4. Cut out pictures from travel magazines, or gather pamphlets and pictures from a travel agency. As you show children each picture, describe its location and tell where it is on a map. Children choose their favorite vacation spots and tell about the things they would like to do there.
Travel/Communication

Art Activities

Vacation Shirts: Cut out the outline of a small tee-shirt on a piece of colored construction paper. Make one for each child. Supply sticky dots, stickers, markers, paints, and crayons with which children may decorate their shirts.

Take-Along Puzzles: Save greeting cards and cut off their back pages. Have children cut the cards into a few simple shapes to make puzzle pieces. Save all of the puzzle pieces in an envelope for long car rides.

Rock Painting: Collect a large variety of rocks, clean them, and hand them to children to decorate. Provide paints and brushes.

Tasty Treats

Fast Food Meal: Contact a local fast food restaurant to get donations of such items as hats, napkins, cups, trays, etc. Serve hamburgers and chips in the donated containers.

Fruity Cereal Necklace: String fruit-flavored cereal on a piece of yarn. Tie the yarn ends together to make a necklace. Take these edible necklaces along on a trip for a snack "on the road."

Books: Vacations

The Happy Lion's Vacation by Louise Fatio. McGraw & Hill, 1967.

See page 120 for Vacations Certificate.

JUNIOR CAMPER AWARD FOR

_____

(CHILD'S NAME)

CAMPING

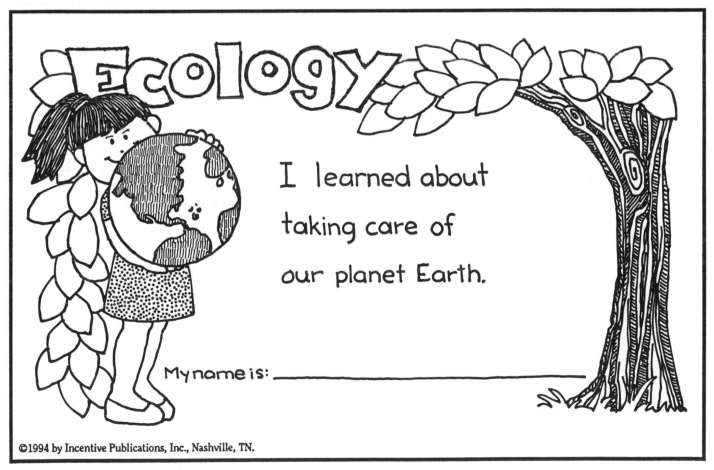

Ecology

I learned about taking care of our planet Earth.

My name is: _____

NIGHT TIME

Our study of nighttime taught me about the phases of the Moon and the beauty of the stars.

My name is:

_____

VACATIONS

I learned about the art of taking a holiday.

My name is: _____

September

Theme	Monday	Tuesday	Wednesday	Thursday	Friday
Beginning of School and Safety	Rules for safety	Share a blanket or cuddle toy that helps you feel safe	Red Day: Wear red like a stop sign	Buddy Day: Bring in a traffic sign shape	Cooking Day: Traffic Sign Cookies
Me–I Am Special	Body Tracing Day	Bring in your very favorite toy to share	Share a picture of yourself	Wear your favorite color today	Cooking Day: Faces
Families	Start making family albums	Bring in a picture of your family	Make a mural of your home and family	Create your family tree	Cooking Day: Family Trees
Autumn	Leaf hunt	Bring in an apple to share	Wear the colors of Autumn: Orange and brown	Squirrel Day: Nut tasting	Cooking Day: Red Applesauce

Extra Days

Extra Day: Share a picture of a grandparent	Extra Day: Bring in a leaf you found on the ground	Extra Day: Share your favorite apple recipe

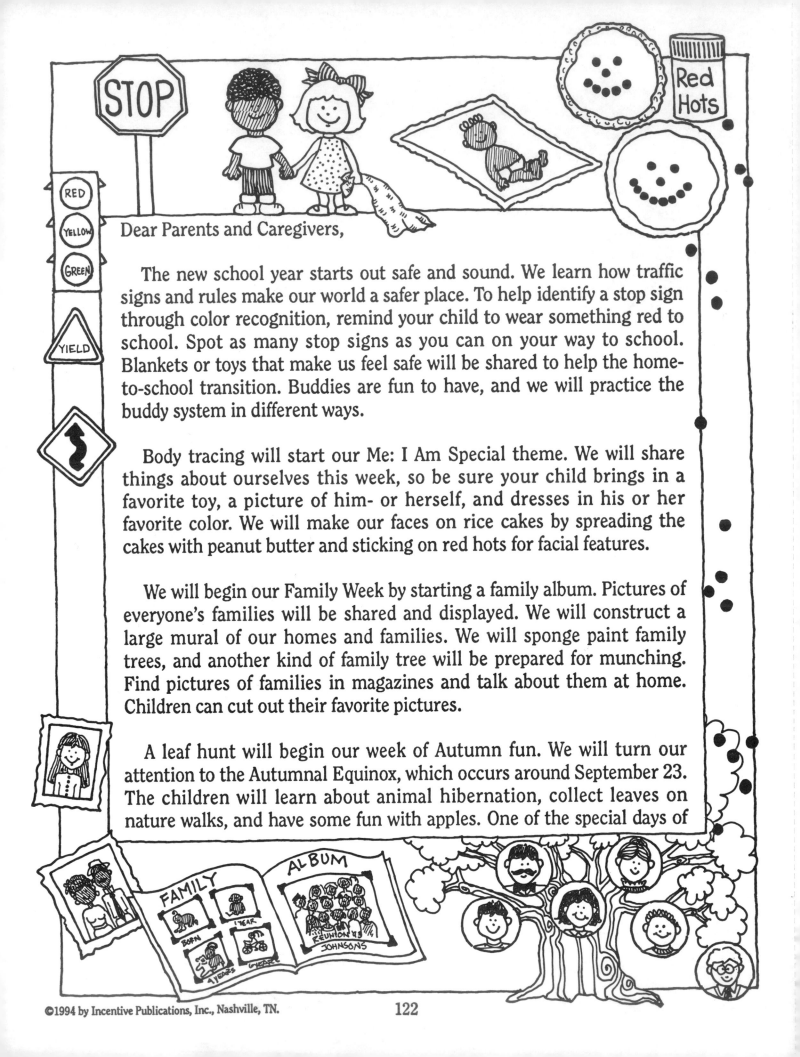

Dear Parents and Caregivers,

The new school year starts out safe and sound. We learn how traffic signs and rules make our world a safer place. To help identify a stop sign through color recognition, remind your child to wear something red to school. Spot as many stop signs as you can on your way to school. Blankets or toys that make us feel safe will be shared to help the home-to-school transition. Buddies are fun to have, and we will practice the buddy system in different ways.

Body tracing will start our Me: I Am Special theme. We will share things about ourselves this week, so be sure your child brings in a favorite toy, a picture of him- or herself, and dresses in his or her favorite color. We will make our faces on rice cakes by spreading the cakes with peanut butter and sticking on red hots for facial features.

We will begin our Family Week by starting a family album. Pictures of everyone's families will be shared and displayed. We will construct a large mural of our homes and families. We will sponge paint family trees, and another kind of family tree will be prepared for munching. Find pictures of families in magazines and talk about them at home. Children can cut out their favorite pictures.

A leaf hunt will begin our week of Autumn fun. We will turn our attention to the Autumnal Equinox, which occurs around September 23. The children will learn about animal hibernation, collect leaves on nature walks, and have some fun with apples. One of the special days of

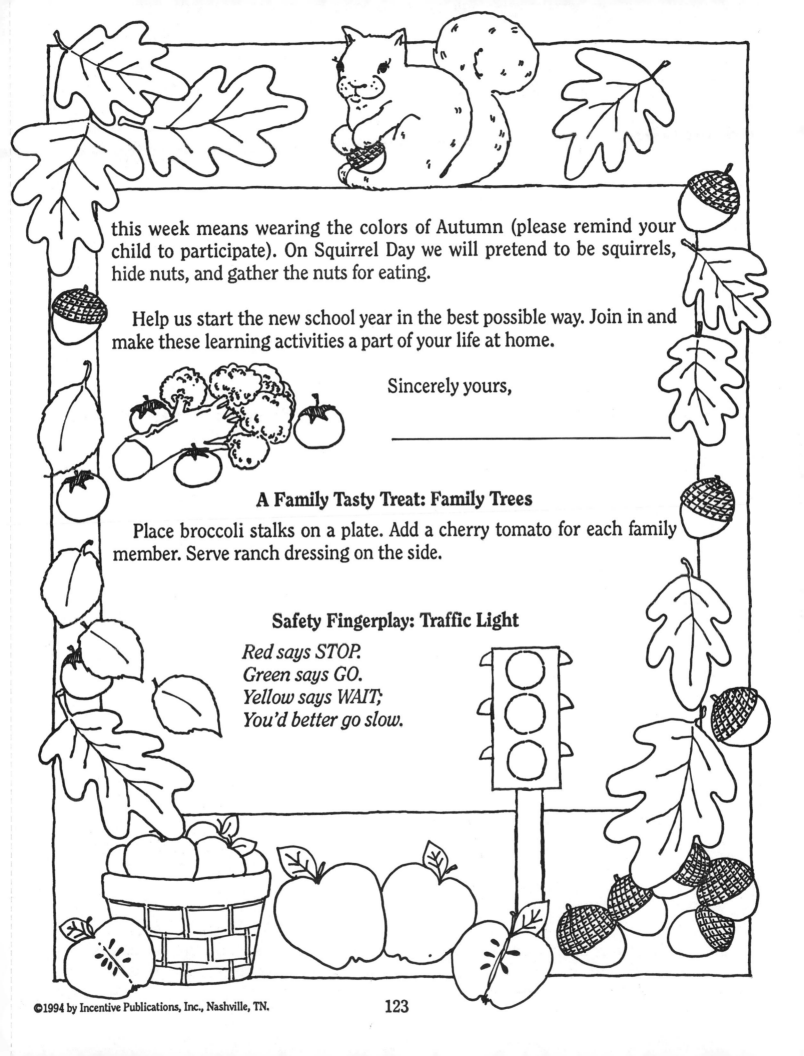

this week means wearing the colors of Autumn (please remind your child to participate). On Squirrel Day we will pretend to be squirrels, hide nuts, and gather the nuts for eating.

Help us start the new school year in the best possible way. Join in and make these learning activities a part of your life at home.

Sincerely yours,

_____

A Family Tasty Treat: Family Trees

Place broccoli stalks on a plate. Add a cherry tomato for each family member. Serve ranch dressing on the side.

Safety Fingerplay: Traffic Light

Red says STOP.
Green says GO.
Yellow says WAIT;
You'd better go slow.

Week 1: Beginning Of School And Safety

Facts

- Rules at school allow children to move freely and safely in their environment.

- Learning traffic signs enriches a child's knowledge of safety.

- Learning the shapes of different traffic signs is fun for children.

Special Days

Monday: Discuss with children that there are special rules designed to help keep them safe when at school. Review your school's safety rules throughout the week.

Tuesday: Children bring in an item that helps them feel safe and protected. Separation from parents can be difficult for the first few days of school. A book which reinforces these feelings is *This Is the Way We Go to School.*

Wednesday: Children wear red like stop signs. Display several stop signs throughout the school. Use stop signs in a tricycle area.

Thursday: It is important that each child is paired with a buddy when taking walks or going on field trips. Introduce the buddy system when practicing the use of stop signs and other traffic signs.

Friday: Make Traffic Sign Cookies (page 125).

Circle Time

1. Each day this week, place masking tape on the floor in a different shape. During Circle Time, have children sit to form the different shapes.
   Gross Motor Skills/Shapes

2. Make shapes of traffic signs and discuss the shapes with the children. They delight in the octagonal shape of the stop sign! Counting its eight sides and mastering the pronunciation of the word "octagon" is quite an accomplishment.
   Traffic Signs/Shape Recognition

3. Construct a large traffic signal out of black tagboard. Make the red, yellow, and green lights out of colored construction paper. Apply sticky strips on the colored circles and have children place the colors on the traffic light in the correct order. As they are

applying the colors to the traffic light, repeat the following poem:

Traffic Light

Red says STOP.
Green says GO.
Yellow says WAIT;
You'd better go slow.

Traffic Signals/Colors

4. Cut out several large traffic sign shapes before Circle Time. Make smaller duplicates for the children to match with your shapes. Play Hap Palmer's song "Shapes" during Circle Time.
Traffic Signs/Shape Recognition

5. Take children on a walk to practice crossing the street, paying attention to traffic signs, and recognizing the colors of traffic lights.
Safety/Color Recognition

Art Activities

Safety Collage: Children cut from magazines pictures pertaining to the first day of school, crossing the street, riding in a car, etc., and combine their pictures to make a giant collage.

Stop Signs: Cut octagons out of white paper and have children paint them red like stop signs.

Play Dough: Make red play dough (see directions below). Allow each child to take some home in a plastic or paper bag.

Buddy Picture: Group children into pairs and ask them to work together to create a picture.

Tasty Treats

Stop Signs: Spread cream cheese that has been colored red with food coloring on crackers.

Traffic Sign Cookies: Allow children to mold refrigerator dough into their favorite shapes.

Play Dough:

- 1 cup flour
- ½ cup salt
- 1 cup water
- 1 tablespoon oil
- 4 teaspoons cream of tartar
- food coloring (any color)

Mix ingredients and cook until a ball forms. Knead dough until soft.

Books: Beginning of School and Safety

The Berenstain Bears Go to School by Stan and Jan Berenstain. Random House, 1978.

First Day in School by Bill Binzen. Doubleday, 1972.

Making Friends by Fred Rogers. Putnam, 1987.

Safety Can Be Fun by Munro Leaf. Lippincott, 1961.

This Is the Way We Go to School by Edith Baer. Scholastic, 1990.

See page 133 for Beginning of School and Safety Certificate.

Week 2: Me–I Am Special

Concepts

- Children need unconditional love. As caregivers, a part of our job is to help children come to understand that each part of them is lovable and acceptable.

- We can assist children in learning to love themselves by helping them realize that each person is unique and special and that every child's ideas and thoughts are important.

- Learning respect for friends, families, and personal belongings is a valuable lesson for a young child.

Special Days

Monday: Trace each child's body on butcher paper. Have children draw their own faces, hair, and clothing.

Tuesday: Each child brings a favorite toy to school and shares why it is special to him or her.

Wednesday: Children bring a picture of themselves to school. Discuss with children how each one of them is unique and special. Point out that each child has a different hair, skin, and eye color.

Thursday: All wear their favorite colors on their clothing today. Point out that everyone likes different colors. Stress that this difference is good; it is what makes each of us an individual. Look through the book *My Book About Me* and ask children questions that relate to the pictures in the book.

Friday: Make Faces for snacktime (page 128).

Circle Time

1. Begin Circle Time with the following fingerplay. Children will have fun when you pass around a mirror and ask them to look at their reflections while completing the sentence: "I am special because . . ."

I Am Special

I'm glad I'm me; I'm special, look and see.
My feet can run and dance and walk.
My ears can hear; my mouth can talk.
My hands and arms can stretch out wide.
My face shows how I feel inside.

Self-Awareness/Poem

2. Make an eye chart on a piece of white tagboard. Write each child's name on the tagboard and ask the children to draw in the colors of their eyes. Throughout the week, have each child point out his or her name and eye color. This activity can be extended by cutting eye colors out of construction paper and asking children to match them with the colors on the eye chart.
Self-Awareness/Color Recognition

3. Replace the words in the song "If You're Happy and You Know It" with your students' names. For example, sing: "If you're Lisa and you know it, clap your hands" or "If you're John and you know it, stamp your feet."
Self-Awareness/Language Development

4. Trace oval shapes on a piece of newsprint and secure to a wall at a height the children can reach. Provide crayons or markers that match the children's hair colors. Each child can color his or her own hair color on one of the oval shapes. Allow each to choose a hair color different from his or her own if desired. It's fun to add facial features.
Self-Awareness/Color Recognition

Art Activities

Eye Collage: Children cut pictures of eyes from magazines and combine them to make a collage.

Me Dolls: Children put faces, hair, clothes, etc., on a large body outline prepared by the teacher. Supply yarn and material scraps for the figure.

Feet Painting: Paint the bottoms of children's feet and have them walk across a large piece of newsprint. Hang the finished product on a wall for all to view.

Lip Prints: Apply lipstick on children's lips and let them make lip prints on sheets of white paper.

Happy Faces: Supply each child with a happy face sticker and a piece of paper. Children draw a picture of something that makes them feel happy.

Tasty Treats

Faces: Spread peanut butter on rice cakes. Apply facial features with red hots.

Bread People: Children knead and design body figures using frozen bread dough. You may prefer to make your own bread recipe instead.

Books: Me–I Am Special

All By Myself by Mercer Mayer. Western Publishing Co., 1983.

Frederick by Leo Lionni. Pantheon Books, 1967.

Leo the Late Bloomer by Robert Krauss. Windmill Books, 1971.

Just Me by Marie Hall Ets. Viking Press, 1965.

My Book About Me by Dr. Seuss. Random House, 1969.

See page 133 for Me–I Am Special Certificate.

Week 3: Families

Facts

- All societies have a family group system.

- When we refer to family, we typically mean a mother, father, sister, and brother; however, over the past few decades family make-up has changed. There are now many single-parent families, and children raised by aunts, uncles, or grandparents. Stress to children that a family is any unit of people who love and care for each other.

Special Days

Monday: Each child constructs a family album by drawing pictures of and telling stories about his or her family members.

Tuesday: Children bring in pictures of their families to share with the class. Read the book *Shoes from Grandpa.*

SEPTEMBER

Wednesday: Children draw pictures of their homes and streets on a large sheet of butcher paper. Hang the mural on a wall for all to view.

Thursday: Each child creates his or her own family tree (see Art Activities below).

Friday: For a healthful snack, make Family Trees using cherry tomatoes and broccoli (page 130).

Circle Time

1. Ask each child to finish the following sentence: "I live in a house with . . ."
   Self-Awareness/Sentence Starter

2. Children act out stories about their family members using paper or other types of dolls. These figures can also be used for counting how many family members each child has. End Circle Time with the following fingerplay:

   Where Is My Family?
   (Sung to the tune of "Where Is Thumpkin?")

   Where is mommy? Where is mommy?
   Here she is. Here she is.
   I love mommy. I love mommy.
   She loves me. She loves me.

   (Continue with daddy, brother, sister, baby, and whole family.)
   Self-Awareness/Family

3. Show children a picture of a family and have each child share what he or she thinks is happening in the picture.
   Family/Interpretation

4. Ask children to share how they get from their houses to the school. Follow this discussion with a presentation of a city map; show children their routes to and from school.
   Self-Awareness/Map Skills

Art Activities

Family Trees: Supply each child with a piece of paper that has a tree shape drawn on it and sponges cut into apple shapes. Have children sponge paint apples on their trees to represent each family member.

Family Collage: Each child cuts a picture of a family from a magazine, glues it on a sheet of paper, and tells a story about the family. Write the story each child dictates next to his or her picture.

Graham Cracker Houses: Apply graham crackers spread with peanut butter to the sides of small milk cartons. Decorate the houses with miniature marshmallows, red hots, and raisins. The peanut butter serves as glue.

Tasty Treats

Family Trees: Place broccoli stalks on a plate. Add a cherry tomato for each family member. Serve ranch dressing on the side.

Sugar Cookie Family: Children cut refrigerator cookie dough into shapes of family members and decorate them with sugar and cinnamon.

Books: Families

Are You My Mother? by P.D. Eastman. Random House, 1960.

The Berenstain Bears' New Baby by Stan and Jan Berenstain. Random House, 1974.

Clifford's Family by Norman Bridwell. Scholastic, 1984.

Just Me and My Mom by Mercer Mayer. Western Publishing Co., 1990.

Shoes from Grandpa by Mem Fox. Orchard Books, 1989.

See page 134 for Families Certificate.

Week 4: Autumn

Facts

- The Autumn Equinox occurs around September 23. This is the time (along with the Spring Equinox) when the hours of darkness and light are approximately equal.
- The season of Autumn season follows the Summer season. During Autumn, the weather turns from hot to chilly.
- Many animals hibernate during Autumn: their heartbeats slow down, and they fall into a very deep sleep that lasts throughout the Winter.

Special Days

Monday: Take a nature walk to collect leaves. Let children walk in pairs using the buddy system. Display the leaves on a wall inside the classroom.

Tuesday: Children share apples they have brought from home. Examine the different kinds of apples and categorize them by size and color. Eat the apples late in the day and read the story *Apple Tree! Apple Tree!* to the children.

Wednesday: Children wear the colors of Autumn today. Fill a basket full of leaves. Ask one child to hold the basket while walking around the playground and dropping a trail of leaves. Other children follow the trail to its end.

Thursday: Hide nuts throughout the school. Children pretend to be squirrels and gather the nuts. End the fun by tasting the nuts that have been discovered.

Friday: Prepare Red Applesauce (page 132).

Circle Time

1. Bring assorted nuts to class and ask children to categorize them by shape, size, and color.
   Matching/Categorizing

2. Bring pictures of hibernating animals to class and discuss the process of hibernation with the children. Make sequencing cards showing the stages of hibernation of bears and squirrels.
   Hibernation/Sequencing

3. Make small, medium, and large apples out of felt material. Cut out a worm shape from green felt. Place the apples on the flannelboard, hiding the worm behind one of the apples. Children guess which apple the worm is hiding behind using the words small, medium, and large.
   Guessing Game/Size Discrimination

4. Cut red and green apples from construction paper. Hand one apple to each child. Ask all of the red apples to stand up, all of the green apples to clap their hands, etc. Present the following fingerplay:

   Apple Green, Apple Red

   Apple green, apple red.
   Apples falling on my head.
   Apple red, apple green.
   You're the best apple I've ever seen.
   Color Recognition/Following Directions

Art Activities

Bear Cave: Cut the entrance to the cave on the side of a small paper cup. Decorate the cup. Color a cotton ball brown with dry tempera paint or use a brown pom-pom to represent the bear.

Scenery Drawing: Take children outdoors to draw pictures of Autumn scenery.

Nature Collage: Children collect leaves, twigs, small pine cones, nuts, etc., to glue onto a piece of tagboard. Show children how to collect items from the ground without damaging the environment.

SEPTEMBER

Apple Prints: Cut an apple in half and dip it in red or green paint. Stamp onto a sheet of paper to make apple prints.

Tasty Treats

Red Applesauce: Mix red cinnamon-flavored candies with purchased applesauce and cook over low heat until candies have dissolved.

Trail Mix: Add nuts that were found on a nature walk to raisins, popcorn, and oat cereal.

Books: Autumn

Apple Tree! Apple Tree! by Mary Blocksma. Children's Press, 1983.

Autumn Story by Jill Barklem. Philomel Books, 1980.

The Seed the Squirrel Dropped by Petie Harris. Prentice-Hall, 1976.

The Story of Johnny Appleseed by Aliki. Prentice-Hall, 1963.

Up a Tree by Ed Young. Harper & Row, 1983.

See page 134 for Autumn Certificate.

October

Theme	Monday	Tuesday	Wednesday	Thursday	Friday
Dinosaurs	Dinosaur Dancing Day	Make a dinosaur village	Measure a dinosaur	Volcano Eruption Day	Cooking Day: Hot Lava
Dinosaurs	Follow the dinosaur prints	Wear a color you think a dinosaur was	Dye dinosaur eggs	Dinosaur Bone Dig	Cooking Day: Dinosaur Bones
Columbus Day and Discoveries	Boat Sail	Find the lost treasure	Set sail to find a new world	Bring in something you've discovered	Cooking Day: Discover new foods
Halloween	Plant magic pumpkin seeds	Ghost Day: Wear a sheet	Pumpkin Decorating Day: Wear orange	Haunted House	Cooking Day: Caramel apples
Extra Days	Extra Day: Make maps as Columbus did	Extra Day: Wear black like a witch	Extra Day: Bobbing for apples		

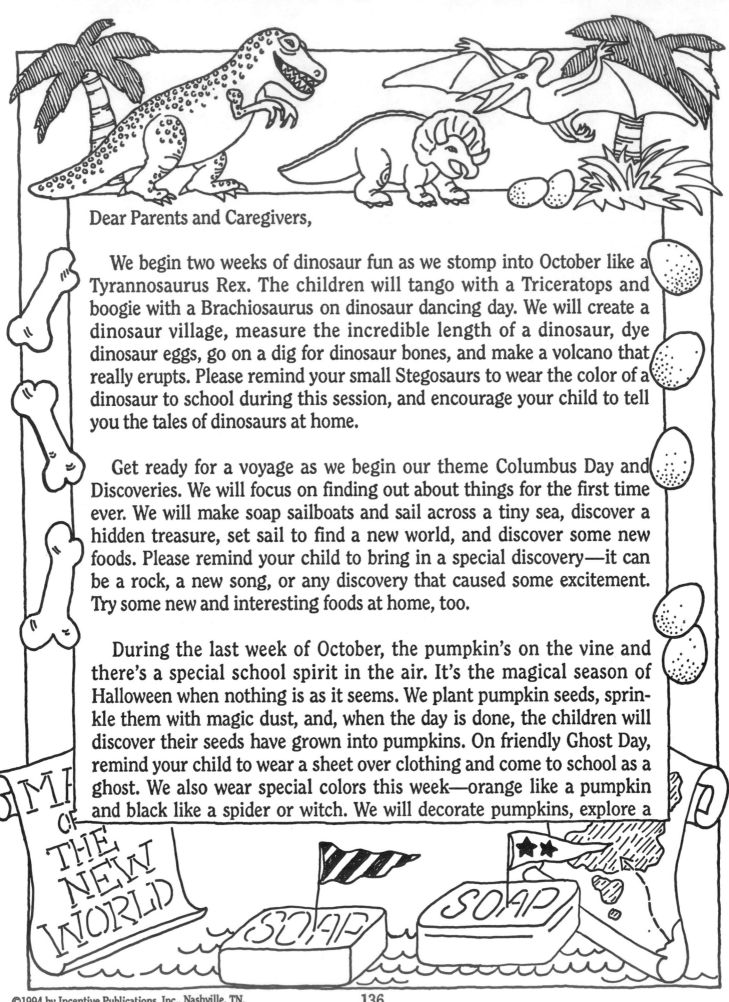

Dear Parents and Caregivers,

We begin two weeks of dinosaur fun as we stomp into October like a Tyrannosaurus Rex. The children will tango with a Triceratops and boogie with a Brachiosaurus on dinosaur dancing day. We will create a dinosaur village, measure the incredible length of a dinosaur, dye dinosaur eggs, go on a dig for dinosaur bones, and make a volcano that really erupts. Please remind your small Stegosaurs to wear the color of a dinosaur to school during this session, and encourage your child to tell you the tales of dinosaurs at home.

Get ready for a voyage as we begin our theme Columbus Day and Discoveries. We will focus on finding out about things for the first time ever. We will make soap sailboats and sail across a tiny sea, discover a hidden treasure, set sail to find a new world, and discover some new foods. Please remind your child to bring in a special discovery—it can be a rock, a new song, or any discovery that caused some excitement. Try some new and interesting foods at home, too.

During the last week of October, the pumpkin's on the vine and there's a special school spirit in the air. It's the magical season of Halloween when nothing is as it seems. We plant pumpkin seeds, sprinkle them with magic dust, and, when the day is done, the children will discover their seeds have grown into pumpkins. On friendly Ghost Day, remind your child to wear a sheet over clothing and come to school as a ghost. We also wear special colors this week—orange like a pumpkin and black like a spider or witch. We will decorate pumpkins, explore a

haunted house, and prepare for Halloween with an important review of safety. We look forward to sharing these great adventures with you. At home, you can make a little jack-o-lantern by drawing a silly face on an orange with a black marker.

Sincerely yours,

_____

A Taste of Dinosaurs: Hot Lava

Heat a can of tomato soup and serve as "hot lava."

Dinosaur Stomp

I'm a big dinosaur stomping my feet.
Can you hear my dinosaur beat?
Stomp your feet fast, stomp your feet slow,
Stomp your feet in circles: go, go, go!

HOT LAVA SOUP

MARK-IT

Week 1: Dinosaurs

Facts

- The word dinosaur comes from the Greek, meaning "monstrous lizard."

- Dinosaurs lived on the Earth for almost 140 million years. They became extinct close to 65 million years ago.

- Fossils are formed when living things make a print in the mud. When the mud turns to stone over the course of millions of years, the print is cast in stone.

- The Brachiosaurus was very, very big. This giant dinosaur was almost 70 feet long and probably weighed 30 tons. The Brachiosaurus was a herbivore (plant-eater). Its long neck was good for reaching plants in high or low places. Its head and mouth were tiny in comparison with its body, so it must have had to spend most of the day eating.

- Tyrannosaurus Rex, often called the "king of tyrants," was a carnivore (meat-eater). This dinosaur was over 45 feet long and 20 feet tall. The Tyrannosaurus had two front legs which were small and almost completely useless. Its back feet, however, were equipped with sharp tearing claws, and its huge head supported massive jaws which allowed the Tyrannosaurus Rex to eat its prey.

- Two rows of thin and sharp bony plates ran along the back of the Stegosaurus. Its tail also had four pointed spikes at its end so that it could rip open its enemies. The Stegosaurus was a herbivore, however, and walked on four legs.

- The Triceratops was a fierce-looking herbivore who had three horns—one on its nose and over each eye. The Triceratops may have roamed the Earth in herds, each weighing about 12 tons and reaching 30 feet.

Special Days

Monday: Play music, and ask children to dance like different dinosaurs. Recite "Dinosaur Stomp," and tell children to repeat the movements suggested in the poem.

Dinosaur Stomp

I'm a big dinosaur stomping my feet.
Can you hear my dinosaur beat?
Stomp your feet fast, stomp your feet slow,
Stomp your feet in circles: go, go, go!

Tuesday: Use a water table or similar container for the dinosaur village. Cover the bottom of the container with sand and add artificial greenery, rocks, a mirror to represent water, and plastic dinosaurs. Display the dinosaur village during Dinosaur Weeks.

Wednesday: Measure the size of a dinosaur in a parking lot or other large area. Cut a piece of string the length of a dinosaur and lay the string along the ground to let children see a dinosaur's actual size. If using pavement, draw the shape of the dinosaur with chalk.

Thursday: Build a large volcano with a crater in its center in your sand area. Pour one-fourth of a box of baking soda into the crater and add vinegar mixed with red food coloring. Watch the volcano erupt as the vinegar meets the baking soda.

Friday: Make Hot Lava for snacktime (page 140).

Circle Time

1. Teach children some dinosaur names, and pass out pictures of several different types of dinosaurs. As each child holds up a picture of one of the dinosaurs, he or she says its name. Some names which are fun for children to learn include Tyrannosaurus Rex, Stegosaurus, Brachiosaurus, Triceratops, Pterodactyl, and Ankylosaurus.
   Dinosaurs/Vocabulary

2. Make a large dinosaur out of newsprint and have each child think of a name for the dinosaur. Write all of their selections on pieces of paper, place them in a large bowl, and choose one. Each day of Dinosaur Week, children share with the dinosaur something new that they have learned.
   Dinosaurs/Communication

3. Attach a large piece of newsprint to the wall at children's eye level. Each day during Circle Time, draw or glue a different dinosaur to the mural. Write the dinosaur's name and how tall it was (e.g. "Triceratops, 30 feet"). Children color the dinosaurs on the mural, adding swamps, foliage, and dinosaur eggs.
   Dinosaurs/Science/Art

4. Distribute a small dinosaur and a plastic egg to each child and tell a little about each dinosaur. Children place the dinosaurs into the eggs while the teacher explains that dinosaurs hatched from eggs.
   Dinosaurs/Science

Art Activities

Volcano Eruption: Cut the shape of a volcano from white construction paper. Mix glue still in the bottle with red food coloring. Children squeeze this "hot lava" onto the paper volcano. Try standing the volcano upright on an easel so the lava runs down the paper.

Dinosaur Place Mats: Cut large dinosaur shapes from colored paper. Each child chooses a dinosaur and colors it with crayons or markers. Write each child's name on his or her dinosaur and laminate it or cover with clear contact paper. During Dinosaur Weeks, let children use these place mats while eating their lunches and snacks.

Water Color Dinosaur: Cut out an outline of a Brachiosaurus from construction paper (one for each child). Children paint their dinosaurs with water that has been colored with food coloring. After the paint dries, they can glue their Brachiosaurus figures onto pieces of blue construction paper. Children add water and foliage to their pictures using markers.

Tasty Treats

Hot Lava: Heat a can of tomato soup and serve as "hot lava."

Tyrannosaurus Rex Terrible Punch: Mix grape, pineapple, and orange juice. Pour in glasses over ice.

Books: Dinosaurs

Dinosaur Garden by Liza Donnelly. Scholastic, 1990.

Dinosaurs by Mary Packard. Simon and Schuster, Inc., 1981.

Patrick's Dinosaurs by Carol Carrick. Clarion Books, 1983.

Tyrannosaurus Was a Beast by Jack Prelutsky. Greenwillow Books, 1988.

See page 147 for Dinosaurs Certificate.

Week 2: Dinosaurs

Special Days

Monday: Cut out dinosaur footprints from construction paper and make tracks throughout the school and on the playground. Children follow the dinosaur footprints to see where they lead.

Tuesday: Children guess the colors dinosaurs were by wearing those colors on their clothing. Read the book *Dinosaur Dream* today.

Wednesday: Children dye hard-boiled eggs. (To make the egg dye, mix water, food coloring, and 1 teaspoon of vinegar.) Fill plastic eggs with small toy dinosaurs and hide these around the playground. Ask children to find the lost dinosaur eggs.

Thursday: Make Dinosaur Bones (Tasty Treats, page 141) and hide them in the sand area. Ask children to search for the buried dinosaur bones.

Friday: Cook Dinosaur Bones for today's snack (Tasty Treats, page 141).

Circle Time

1. Draw several different-colored circles on a piece of newsprint and place the newsprint in the center of the group. Give each child a plastic dinosaur that corresponds with one of the colored circles on the newsprint. Call out a color and ask all children whose dinosaurs correspond with that color to place them on the proper circle.
Dinosaurs/Color Discrimination

2. Children pretend to be any dinosaur they wish. Ask children which dinosaur they are, how it feels to be that dinosaur, if they are carnivorous or herbivorous, etc. Children move about as they feel dinosaurs may have moved.
Dinosaurs/Imaginative Play

3. Give each child a toy or construction paper dinosaur. Ask children to place their dinosaurs on their laps, feet, heads, hands, backs, stomachs, etc.
Dinosaurs/Following Directions

4. Cut out many small dinosaurs from construction paper and place them throughout the classroom. During Circle Time, describe the location of one of the dinosaurs (e.g., "Lisa, can you find the dinosaur hanging upside down on the wall?"). When the child finds the hidden dinosaur, he or she describes what the dinosaur looks like. Allow each child an opportunity to locate and describe a dinosaur.
Dinosaurs/Communication

Art Activities

Dino Footprints: Cut a potato in half and carve out a footprint in the center of the potato to be used as a stamp. Make one for each child. Children dab their potatoes in tempera paint and stamp footprints onto paper.

Dinosaur Fossils: Press plastic dinosaurs into clay to make fossil prints of their heads, bodies, and feet.

Dinosaur Printing: Collect different dinosaur cookie cutters and pass them out to the children who dip them into pans of paint and make dinosaur prints on white paper.

Tasty Treats

Dinosaur Bones: Mix together 1 package of yeast, 1½ cups of warm water, 1 tablespoon of sugar, and 1 tablespoon of salt in a large bowl. Stir in 4 cups of flour and knead until smooth. Shape into dinosaur bones and brush with egg white. Bake in an oven at 425 degrees for 15 minutes.

Herbivore Snack: Cut carrots, celery, broccoli, and cauliflower into pieces. Dip vegetables in ranch dressing.

Books: Dinosaurs

After the Dinosaurs by Stan Berenstain. Random House, 1988.

Curious George and the Dinosaur by Margaret and H. A. Rey. Houghton Mifflin Co., 1989.

Dinosaur Dream by Robin Michal Koontz. Putnam, 1988.

The Dinosaur Who Lived in My Backyard by B. G. Hennessy. Viking Kestrel, 1988.

See page 147 for Dinosaurs Certificate.

Week 3: Columbus Day And Discoveries

Facts

- In 1492, an Italian-born explorer named Christopher Columbus landed in the Americas and opened the lands of the Western Hemisphere to the culture of Europe. Columbus had great courage and imagination. He defied the popular belief that the world was flat and sailed westward to discover new lands.

- Columbus set sail from Spain on August 3, 1492. He was sailing west in hopes of finding a new route to India. His three ships were called the *Pinta, Niña,* and *Santa Maria.*

- Columbus's three ships sailed the Atlantic Ocean for 72 days before he and his crew reached what is now the Caribbean Islands. He thought he had reached the East Indies.

- In 1892, President Benjamin Harrison declared October 12 an American national holiday (Columbus Day) to celebrate Columbus's discovery of America.

Special Days

Monday: Children sail soap boats in a water table or wading pool. Soap boats can be made by using bars of hotel soap, or by cutting larger bars of soap into fourths. Add a toothpick with a paper sail that has a child's name on it to each soap boat.

Tuesday: Make a treasure box by gluing gold pieces made of construction paper and glitter onto a small school box or cigar box. Place gold pieces in the treasure box and bury it in the sand area. Design a treasure map leading to the box. Children use shovels to dig for the treasure box.

Wednesday: Cut a boat shape from construction paper and attach a popsicle stick to its bottom. Attach a large piece of blue tagboard between two chairs. Cut a slit in the middle of the tagboard and insert the boat in the slit. Move the boat across the tagboard when discussing how Columbus sailed across the ocean.

OCTOBER

Thursday: Children bring to school something new and wonderful they have recently discovered.

Friday: Introduce children to new and different foods (see Tasty Treats below for suggestions).

Circle Time

1. Draw a boat on a large chalkboard. Children take turns drawing themselves in the boat. Draw land on the chalkboard near the boat and ask children to pretend they are on a boat ride to discover new lands. Let each draw something he or she thinks would be in this new land and tell about it.
    Discovery/Imaginative Play

2. Gather many small boxes with lids. Put items such as rocks, cotton balls, barrettes, pencils, feathers, and paper inside each of the boxes. Each child chooses a box, opens it, and discovers what is inside. Then, each child thinks of unusual ways the item could be used.
    Discovery/Creative Thinking

3. There are many types of discoveries, such as the discovery of electricity and the light bulb. Benjamin Franklin is noted for his experiments with electricity; his experiments with a kite in a thunderstorm demonstrated that lightning is electricity. Thomas Edison engineered the first successful light bulb. Bring to Circle Time a small lamp and a light bulb. Show children the small wire in the bulb called the filament. Plug in the lamp so that it lights up. Explain that when electricity reaches the filament, it makes the wire so hot that it glows with light.
    Science/Electricity

4. Provide a globe for the children to examine. Trace Columbus's route with your fingers for children to observe. Ask children to pretend that they are on the voyage with Columbus. Ask them how it would feel to be traveling so many years ago, what it would be like during a storm, if they would miss their families and friends left behind, etc.
    Globe Skills/Communication

Art Activities

Map: Cut a jagged shape from a brown paper bag; this will serve as a map that children can decorate and draw directions to a buried treasure.

Columbus Hats: Glue sequins and feathers onto 9" x 12" pieces of construction paper. Assist children in folding the paper into cone shapes and stapling it to fit their heads.

Tasty Treats

Discover New Foods: Provide exotic foods such as jicama, goat cheese, kiwi fruit, yellow peppers, turnips, mangos, lemon cucumbers, etc.

OCTOBER

Gold Pieces: Cut circle shapes out of slices of American cheese. Serve on crackers.

Books: Columbus Day and Discoveries

Columbus Day by Paul Showers. Crowell, 1965.

See page 148 for Columbus Day And Discoveries Certificate.

Week 4: Halloween

Facts

- Halloween is celebrated in America on October 31, the evening before All Saints Day, or Allhallows. In recent years, Halloween has been celebrated by children "trick or treating" and wearing costumes.

- Halloween as we know it came from a celebration of the Celtic people who believed that night spirits roamed the planet to play tricks on humans. The Celts wore costumes and carved jack-o-lanterns on this evening to protect them from the night spirits.

- Halloween is a night of pretend and fun. Safety needs to be emphasized and reinforced on this special night.

Special Days

Monday: Children put pumpkin seeds in the ground and sprinkle them with magic dust (cornstarch). Flag each child's pumpkin seed with a popsicle stick or tongue depressor that has his or her name written on it. When children check their pumpkin seeds at the end of the day, they will discover that their seeds have magically grown into pumpkins.

Tuesday: Children come to school dressed as ghosts. A ghost (made from a stuffed white sheet) sitting at the door can greet children as they come in the classroom.

Wednesday: Children decorate their pumpkins with markers, yarn, fabric scraps, and glue.

Thursday: Create a haunted house from appliance boxes. Children can paint the boxes black and hang paper spiders, bats, and ghosts in them. Children crawl through the boxes and pretend to be afraid.

Friday: Make caramel apples (page 146).

Circle Time

1. Gather a large kettle and a spoon and pretend you are making a witches' brew. Ask children to look around the classroom for funny or odd objects to add to the brew. Children name their objects before adding them to the kettle. Pretend to eat the brew when it is finished. Share the book *The Witch Next Door* today.
Imaginative Play/Literature

2. Hang pumpkins made from orange construction paper on a wall near your Circle Time area. Hang as many pumpkins as there are days left until Halloween. Each day, a different child draws a face on one of the pumpkins using a black marker and counts the days left until Halloween.
Art/Counting

3. Cut five pumpkins from orange felt and a small bat from black felt and hang them on the flannelboard. Assign each pumpkin a number between one and five. Glue black dots on each of the pumpkins to represent its number. Hide the bat behind one of the pumpkins. Children guess which pumpkin the bat is behind by calling out the number of dots on that pumpkin.
Guessing Game/Number Recognition

4. Draw black eyes on navy beans to make small ghosts. Place the beans in a container. Children count out a specified number of ghosts.
Math/Counting

5. Cut pumpkins of different colors from construction paper or tagboard. Use these pumpkins to tell a story. Begin the story by telling the children that the orange pumpkin was very hungry and so ate a banana and turned yellow. The pumpkin then ate an apple and turned red. Continue until all of the colors have been mentioned. To end the story, ask children what food the pumpkin would need to eat to turn orange again.
Colors/Creative Thinking

Art Activities

Scary Picture: Distribute construction paper and markers to children and ask them to draw pictures of something they find scary.

Pumpkins: Each child receives an orange and uses a permanent black marker to draw a jack-o-lantern face. Display the "pumpkins" or have them for a snack.

Pumpkins on the Vine: Cut pumpkins in various shapes and sizes from orange construction paper. Children sponge paint the pumpkins with orange tempera paint that has been lightened with white tempera. (Paint should be lighter in color than the construction paper.) Hang the pumpkins on the wall with thin strips of twisted brown paper to give the appearance of pumpkins hanging on a vine.

Tasty Treats

Caramel Apples: Melt a package of caramels in a saucepan. Attach apples to popsicle sticks and allow children to dip their apples in the melted caramel. Cool on waxed paper before eating.

Orange Milk and Cocoa Treats: Make Orange Milk by adding orange food coloring. To make Cocoa Treats, melt ¼ cup of margarine or butter over low heat. Add 4 cups of miniature marshmallows, and stir until melted. Remove from heat. Add 6 cups of chocolate-flavored cereal and stir until well-coated. Using a butter spatula or waxed paper press, transfer mixture into a 13" x 9" buttered pan. Cut into squares when cool.

Books: Halloween

Clifford's Halloween by Norman Bridwell. Scholastic, 1986.

The Halloween Performance by Felicia Bond. Scholastic, 1983.

How Spider Saved Halloween by Robert Kraus. Scholastic, 1973.

Popcorn by Frank Asch. Parents' Magazine Press, 1979.

The Witch Next Door by Norman Bridwell. Scholastic, 1986.

See page 148 for Halloween Certificate.

DINOSAURS

_____ asaurus
(child's name)

is
a
friend
of
dinosaurs.

DINOSAURS

I covered the enormous subject
of dinosaurs by playing
counting games, hunting bones
and dyeing dinosaur eggs.

My name is:

_____

Columbus Day and Discoveries

I made many new discoveries.

My name is: _____

HALLOWEEN

I had a ghostly good time during Halloween week.

My name is:

_____

November

Theme	Monday	Tuesday	Wednesday	Thursday	Friday
Nursery Rhymes	Pail of water races	Humpty Dumpty egg toss	Jump over the candlestick	Bring in an old shoe	Cooking Day: Curds and Whey
Fairy Tales	Catch the gingerbread man	Visit our gingerbread house	Wear red like Little Red Riding Hood	Cinderella shoe fitting	Cooking Day: Gingerbread
Nutrition	Sandwich-making bar	Bring in a picture of a nutritious food	Fruit juice stand	Bring in a piece of fruit to share	Cooking Day: Potato Bar
Thanksgiving	Totem building	Pilgrim hat making	Thanksgiving Feast: Join the Native Americans and Pilgrims	Turkey Trot	Pow wow and face painting
Extra Days	Extra Day: Make Native American headbands	Extra Day: Share your favorite shape	Extra Day: Pretend you are a Pilgrim. How do you feel in the new land?		

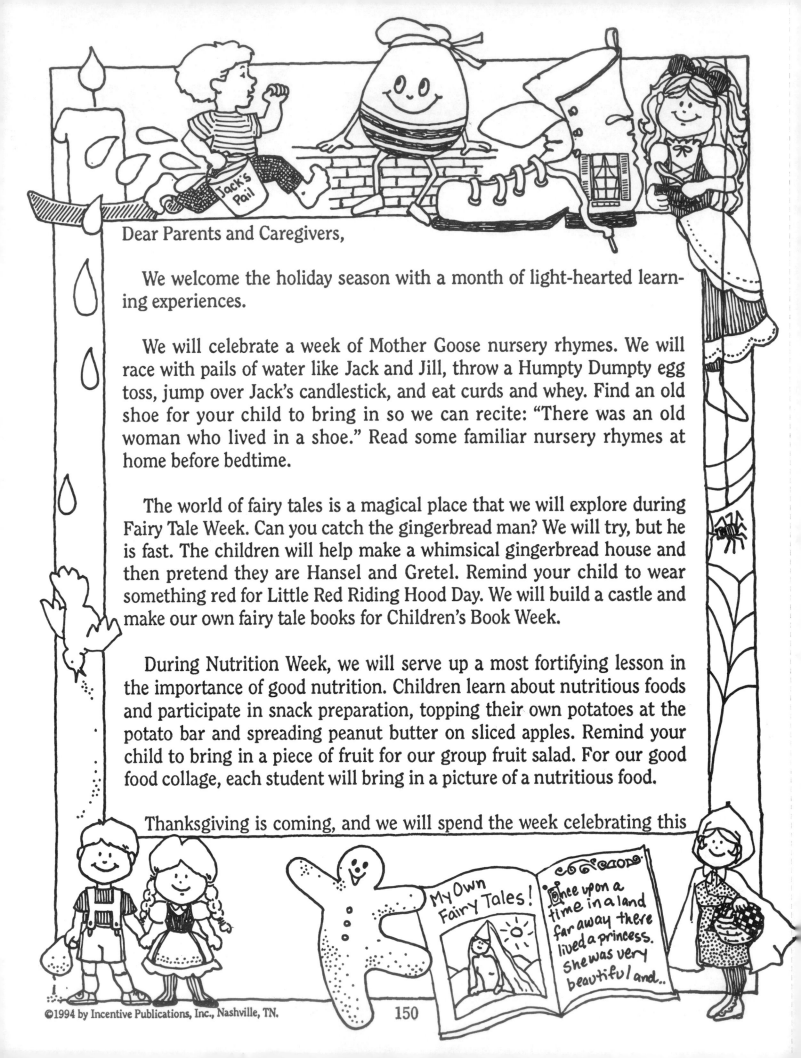

Dear Parents and Caregivers,

We welcome the holiday season with a month of light-hearted learning experiences.

We will celebrate a week of Mother Goose nursery rhymes. We will race with pails of water like Jack and Jill, throw a Humpty Dumpty egg toss, jump over Jack's candlestick, and eat curds and whey. Find an old shoe for your child to bring in so we can recite: "There was an old woman who lived in a shoe." Read some familiar nursery rhymes at home before bedtime.

The world of fairy tales is a magical place that we will explore during Fairy Tale Week. Can you catch the gingerbread man? We will try, but he is fast. The children will help make a whimsical gingerbread house and then pretend they are Hansel and Gretel. Remind your child to wear something red for Little Red Riding Hood Day. We will build a castle and make our own fairy tale books for Children's Book Week.

During Nutrition Week, we will serve up a most fortifying lesson in the importance of good nutrition. Children learn about nutritious foods and participate in snack preparation, topping their own potatoes at the potato bar and spreading peanut butter on sliced apples. Remind your child to bring in a piece of fruit for our group fruit salad. For our good food collage, each student will bring in a picture of a nutritious food.

Thanksgiving is coming, and we will spend the week celebrating this holiday. We will learn about the first Thanksgiving feast in 1621, study Native American artifacts, and make totem poles and Pilgrim hats. Festivities include a turkey trot, a pow wow, and face painting. The highlight of the week will be a glorious feast when we acknowledge all the good things in life and share our food and friendship.

Sincerely yours,

_____

Nursery Rhyme Tasty Treat: Candlesticks

Place a pineapple ring on a plate. Cut a banana into thirds and put one third into the hole in the pineapple ring. Top with a cherry (the flame).

Poem: Thanksgiving

The family gathers around,
Waiting for the turkey, fat and round.
Pumpkin pie and cranberries, too,
Have been prepared for me and you.
This is the day we all share
And think about how much we care.
What holiday is it?

Week 1: Nursery Rhymes

Facts

- A nursery rhyme is a short, rhymed poem for children.

- Mother Goose rhymes are anonymous nursery rhymes or verse. They are traditional, brief verses learned by most children in English-speaking parts of the world.

Special Days

Monday: Run relay races with pails of water. (Sand buckets work well because they are light in weight.)

Tuesday: Hardboil eggs for an egg toss. Group children into pairs and let each pair toss an egg back and forth.

Wednesday: Provide a candlestick for children to jump over. As each child jumps over the candlestick, the others recite the nursery rhyme: "Jack, be nimble; Jack, be quick. Jack, jump over the candlestick."

Thursday: Children examine old shoes which are displayed in a special area of the classroom. Recite the nursery rhyme "There Was an Old Woman Who Lived in a Shoe" during Circle Time.

Friday: Eat curds and whey like Little Miss Muffet (page 153).

Circle Time

1. Bring in an old clock and a mouse finger puppet and recite the nursery rhyme "Hickory, Dickory, Dock" while children clap their hands to the beat. Let each child take a turn making the mouse run up and down the clock.
   Nursery Rhyme/Rhythmic Play

2. Recite familiar and new nursery rhymes with the children. On the chalkboard or posterboard have the children draw pictures of how they think each nursery rhyme might look. Allow each child to tell a story about his or her picture.
   Art/Storytelling

3. Read aloud the nursery rhyme "There Was an Old Woman Who Lived in a Shoe." Instead of the line "we whipped them all soundly," substitute the phrase "she kissed (or hugged) them all soundly." Also bring to Circle Time a shoe and ten small dolls. Place all of the dolls in the shoe and ask each child how many children they think live in the shoe. After all of the children have answered, count the dolls in the shoe—one by one. Then ask each child to count out a certain number of dolls and place them

back in the shoe. Ask the children how it would feel to live in a shoe.
Math/Counting/Imaginative Thinking

4. Recite "Little Bo-Peep":

> *Little Bo-Peep has lost her sheep,*
> *And can't tell where to find them;*
> *Leave them alone, and they'll come home,*
> *Wagging their tails behind them.*

Cut the outlines of sheep from white felt and distribute one to each child. Instruct the children to hide their sheep somewhere near where they are sitting and then ask each one where his or her sheep is hiding. "Is it hiding on your knee? Is it hiding on top of your head? Is it hiding behind you?" After each child's sheep has been found, have him or her place it on the flannelboard. Once all of the sheep have been found, count them on the flannelboard as a group.
Guessing Game/Counting

5. Act out the "Little Miss Muffet" nursery rhyme using a chair, a dish, and a spoon for props. Allow each child a chance to be Miss Muffet and the spider.

> *Little Miss Muffet sat on a tuffet,*
> *Eating some curds and whey.*
> *Along came a spider, and sat down beside her,*
> *And frightened Miss Muffet away.*

Nursery Rhyme/Self-Expression

Art Activities

Humpty Dumpty: Hardboil one egg for each child. Cut felt arms and legs for children to glue onto their eggs. Children also draw faces on their eggs using colored markers.

Mother Goose: Children mold clay into goose shapes. Provide feathers for children to stick into the clay.

Mary's Lamb: Cut sheep outlines from tagboard. Distribute one to each child. Children decorate their sheep using cotton balls for the wool. Glue on wiggly eyes for a special effect.

Tasty Treats

Curds and Whey: Serve cottage cheese as curds and whey. Fruit or vegetables can be added to make the dish more appetizing.

Candlesticks: Place a pineapple ring on a plate. Cut a banana into thirds and put one third into the hole in the pineapple ring. Top with a cherry (the flame).

Patty Cake Cupcakes: Bake cupcakes from a packaged cake mix and top with canned frosting. Place candy sprinkles on the tops of the cupcakes. As you prepare the cupcakes with the children, recite "Patty Cake."

Books: Nursery Rhymes

Favorite Nursery Rhymes by Diane Namm. Little Simon, 1986.

Read-Aloud Rhymes for the Very Young selected by Jack Prelutsky. Alfred A. Knopf, 1986.

The Real Mother Goose illustrated by Blanche Fisher Wright. Rand McNally and Co., 1916.

The Silly Mother Hubbard by Leonard P. Kessler. Garrard Publisher Co., 1980.

Three Little Kittens Lost Their Mittens by Elaine Livermore. Houghton Mifflin, 1979.

See page 161 for Nursery Rhymes Certificate.

Week 2: Fairy Tales

Facts

- A fairy tale is a fantastic story about giants, queens, kings, princesses, dragons, magical deeds, etc.

Special Days

Monday: Play a game of tag and assign one child to be the gingerbread man. The gingerbread man runs as fast as he or she can while the other children try to catch him or her. Children also pretend to be the other characters in the fairy tale "The Gingerbread Man."

Tuesday: Use an appliance box to create the gingerbread house from *Hansel and Gretel*. Children can decorate the box with paint and act out the story.

Wednesday: Children wear the color red on their clothing for Little Red Riding Hood Day. Take a walk through the woods to try to find the wolf.

Thursday: Act out the story of *Cinderella*. Provide a shoe for the children to try on. (A clear plastic pump would look like Cinderella's glass slipper.)

Friday: Bake some gingerbread, but don't let it run away like the gingerbread man did (page 155).

Circle Time

1. Fill a large picnic basket with different objects or pieces of plastic food. Children take turns placing their hands in the basket, feeling an object, and guessing what Little Red Riding Hood has in her picnic basket.
   Sense of Touch/Guessing Game

2. Read or tell the story of *Cinderella*. Then make a magic wand using a dowel rod, tagboard star, glitter, and ribbon. Pass the magic wand around the class and ask children to pretend to change or make something appear by magic.
   Fairy Tale/Imaginative Play

3. Read or tell the story of "The Three Pigs." After the story has been read, have the children act out the various roles. Make simple masks for the three pigs and the wolf, attaching tongue depressors to the masks so that they are easy to hold. You may decide that masks are not necessary, as children have vivid imaginations.
   Fairy Tale/Role Playing

4. Children's Book Week is the second week of November. This is a great time to have children invent a fairy tale of their own. After reading aloud the story of "Jack and the Beanstalk," ask children to draw pictures in response to questions about the story. You may want to ask what they might find after climbing the beanstalk into the clouds, how they would outwit the giant, etc. Then have them tell stories to match their pictures. Put all of the pictures and stories together in book form and display in a special place.
   Drawing/Creative Writing/Publishing

Art Activities

Castle: Bring in many different sizes of empty thread spools. Children make a castle by stacking and gluing spools together on a small cardboard or tagboard base. When the castle has dried, children decorate it with paint that has been mixed with glitter.

Crowns: Cut crown shapes from tagboard and distribute one to each child. Children decorate their crowns with sequins, beads, stickers, and crayons. When the crowns have dried, staple them to fit each child's head.

Snow White's Apple Prints: Cut apples in half. Dip an apple half in red or green tempera paint and press onto a piece of paper.

Tasty Treats

Gingerbread: Make gingerbread from a mix. Serve warm with milk.

Little Pigs House of Sticks: Each child builds a house from pretzel sticks.

Books: Fairy Tales

Cinderella illustrated by Paul Galdone. McGraw Hill, 1978.

The Gingerbread Boy illustrated by Paul Galdone. Seabury Press, 1975.

Hansel and Gretel retold and illustrated by James Marshall. Dial Books, 1990.

The Princess and the Pea by Hans Christian Anderson. Translated by Anthea Bell. Picture Book Studio, 1987.

The Random House Book of Fairy Tales adapted by Amy Ehrlich. Random House, 1985.

See page 161 for Fairy Tales Certificate.

Week 3: Nutrition

Facts

- Children learn by imitation; therefore, it is helpful for them to eat snacks or meals with parents or teachers. To help with feeding skills, provide a small glass, a straight spoon with a small handle, and a comfortable chair.

- Children seem to need to eat many snacks throughout the day. Try offering a morning and afternoon snack each day.

- Some nutritious snacks are pieces of cheese with crackers, cottage cheese, fresh fruits, and fresh vegetables.

- Children like to be involved in preparing their own snacks. Allow them to help make their snacks an attractive presentation.

Special Days

Monday: Spread a tablecloth on a long table to make a sandwich bar. Slice bread and cheese into various shapes and set out lettuce, tomatoes, and bean sprouts. Children make their own sandwiches from the items at the sandwich bar. They will have fun matching cheese shapes to their pieces of bread.

Tuesday: Children share pictures of a nutritious food and choose places on the wall on which to hang them.

Wednesday: Make a fruit juice stand by placing a table and chairs outside. Add to the front of the stand a poster drawn by the children. Provide oranges, lemons, and juice squeezers for the children to make the juice. After sugar and water have been added, children can pour the fruit juice into glasses for their customers.

Thursday: Make a group fruit salad using all of the fruit that children bring from home. Play "Apple, Apple, Orange" by sitting in a circle and playing the familiar children's game of "Duck, Duck, Goose," substituting it with the words "apple" and "orange."

Friday: Children prepare their own potatoes at a potato bar (see page 158 for suggestions).

Circle Time

1. Share the book *Bread, Bread, Bread* and bring a variety of breads to Circle Time. (Some suggestions include raisin bread, pumpernickel, whole wheat, and dill.) Discuss with children how breads supply us with needed energy and give us protein when eaten with a legume (such as peanut butter) for body building and repair. Children choose which breads they want to taste and, if desired, spread margarine on the breads they eat.
   Nutrition/Literature

2. Bring several kinds of fresh fruits and vegetables to Circle Time. Classify the fruits and vegetables for children and then mix them up and allow children to try to classify them again.
   Nutrition/Classification

3. Gather two small boxes; draw a happy face on one of the boxes and a sad face on the other. Collect pictures of foods that are and are not nutritious and have children place the pictures of the nutritious foods in the box with the happy face and the pictures of the unhealthy foods in the box with the sad face.
   Nutrition/Classification

4. Write each child's name on a piece of posterboard. During Circle Time, ask each child to state his or her favorite food and draw a picture of it next to his or her name. Throughout the week, children recall each other's favorite food.
   Self-Awareness/Memory

5. Place different kinds of fruit in a bag. Each child takes a turn feeling a piece of fruit in the bag (without looking at it) and trying to guess what it is. Each child can eat the piece of fruit he or she chooses. Recite the following poem:

   ### Red Apple, Red Apple

   Red apple, red apple who do you see?
   I see a yellow banana looking at me.
   Yellow banana, yellow banana who do you see?
   I see a purple grape looking at me.

   (Continue with green pear, orange orange, etc.)
   Sense of Touch/Guessing

Art Activities

Good Food Collage: Children cut or tear out pictures of nutritious foods from magazines and glue them on a large piece of paper to make a collage. Display on a wall during Nutrition Week.

Bowl of Cereal: Cut bowl shapes from pieces of construction paper and supply one to each child. Provide nutritious cereals for children to glue onto their bowls.

Place Setting Tracing: Place a plate, cup, fork, and spoon on a piece of construction paper (one per child). Children trace these objects onto their pieces of paper and add food to their plates.

Potato Heads: Distribute small potatoes to each child. Provide wiggly eyes, pieces of yarn, fabric scraps, permanent markers, and glue, and let each child create his or her own Mr. or Mrs. Potato.

Tasty Treats

Potato Bar: Bake potatoes until tender. Cut each potato into fourths and serve with various toppings (cheese, broccoli, sour cream, margarine, beans, etc.).

Apple Slices and Peanut Butter: Slice apples into wedges. Children use popsicle sticks to spread peanut butter onto their apple pieces.

Books: Nutrition

Bread, Bread, Bread by Ann Morris. Scholastic, 1989.

Chicken Soup with Rice by Maurice Sendak. Scholastic, 1962.

Gregory, the Terrible Eater by Mitchell Sharmat. Four Winds Press, 1980.

Jam by Margaret Mahy. Trumpet Club, 1985.

Pancakes for Breakfast by Tomie dePaola. Harcourt Brace Jovanovich, 1978.

See page 162 for Nutrition Certificate.

Week 4: Thanksgiving

Facts

- Thanksgiving was first observed in the Autumn of 1621 by the Pilgrims of Plymouth Colony. It was a three-day feast to give thanks for a bountiful harvest. Chief Massosoit and his Native American tribe celebrated with the Pilgrims.

- Americans celebrate this holiday by giving thanks for all of the blessings of the year. Traditionally, families gather for a large dinner on this day.

- A traditional Thanksgiving dinner consists of turkey served with dressing or stuffing, sweet potatoes, mashed potatoes, cranberries, and pumpkin pie for desert.

Special Days

Monday: Children cover coffee cans with construction paper and decorate them with colored markers. The cans are then stacked to make a totem pole.

Tuesday: Make Pilgrim hats by cutting bands and squares from black construction paper. Affix one square to the center of a band and staple the band to fit a child's head. An aluminum foil buckle can also be added.

Wednesday: Decorate your school or classroom with festive decorations for the Thanksgiving feast. If you facility has adequate equipment, cook the dinner at school. If not, have parents help prepare the food at home. You may want to consider sharing your feast with the elderly from a nearby nursing home.

Thursday: Children become turkeys by tucking colored feathers in the backs of their waistbands. They can participate in a turkey trot by skipping around the classroom or playground and gobbling like turkeys. Share the funny story of the *Turkey on the Loose*.

Friday: Children make brightly colored Native American headbands from construction paper and feathers and paint each other's faces. Form a large circle in which to dance and play drums.

Circle Time

1. Ask children to close their eyes and pretend to be present for America's first Thanksgiving. Ask children to name the foods they are having for dinner, who their dinner guests are, etc. As a follow-up to this activity, ask children to express themselves on paper by drawing the different scenes they imagined. Allow them to tell you about their drawings. Recite the following Thanksgiving poem:

   ### Thanksgiving

   The family gathers around,
   Waiting for the turkey, fat and round.
   Pumpkin pie and cranberries, too,
   Have been prepared for me and you.
   This is the day we all share
   And think about how much we care.
   What holiday is it?

   Imaginative Thinking/Drawing

2. Attach a large piece of newsprint to the wall at children's eye level. During Circle Time, share with children some of the things for which you are thankful. Ask each child to share something for which he or she feels thankful and draw it on the piece of newsprint. Write what each child has shared next to its picture on the newsprint.
   Art/Self-Expression

3. Place a square piece of paper in the center of your Circle Time area. Provide paper feathers cut from various colors of construction paper. Allow each child to place a blue feather in the center of the square, red feathers on the four corners, etc.
   Color Discrimination/Following Directions

4. Bring a variety of Native American artifacts to Circle Time. Some ideas include pottery, sand painting, head dresses, clothing, jewelry, and moccasins. Let children carefully examine and discuss the artifacts.
   Native American Study/Artifacts

5. Tell children that Native Americans used to draw pictures and use symbols to tell stories. Then make up a Native American story. As you tell the story, draw pictures on a chalkboard or large piece of paper. Let each child have a chance to tell and draw his or her own story.
   Storytelling/Drawing

Art Activities

Petroglyphs: Children draw pictures on play dough or clay as Native Americans have done on rocks or in caves. Prepare children for this activity by showing them pictures of some actual petroglyphs.

Thankful Collage: Provide magazines from which children can cut pictures of things for which they are thankful. Glue these pictures on a large paper cornucopia.

Native American Bracelets: Slit a toilet paper roll lengthwise and then cut in half. The halves of the roll make two bracelets. Distribute bracelets to the children who decorate them with brightly colored markers and wear on their wrists.

Tepees: Cut many large circles from construction paper and distribute one to each child. Children color one side of their circles and then make them into cone shapes and staple.

Tasty Treats

Totem Poles: Spread peanut butter on the tops and bottoms of marshmallows and stack together.

Pumpkin Pie: Buy a prepared pie crust and a can or box of pumpkin pie mix. Children can assist in preparing and baking the pie according to package directions.

Cranberry Relish: Mix in a food processor one bag of cranberries and a peeled orange. Add a cup of sugar to the mixture. You can also use a meat grinder for this process; children enjoy turning the handle.

Books: Thanksgiving

Arrow to the Sun by Gerald McDermott. Viking Press, 1974

Indian Bunny by Ruth Bornstein. Scholastic, 1973.

The Legend of the Bluebonnet retold and illustrated by Tomie dePaola. Putnam, 1983.

Little Bear's Thanksgiving by Janice Brustlein. Lothrop, Lee & Shepard, 1967.

Turkey on the Loose by Sylvie Wickstrom. Dial Books, 1990.

See page 162 for Thanksgiving Certificate.

NURSERY

_____ be nimble
(child's name)
_____ be quick
(child's name)
_____ jumped
(child's name)

over the candlestick.

RHYMES

FAIRY TALES

I traveled to the world of fairy tales.

My name is:

_____

MAGIC CARPET AIR

NUTRITION

After a week of studying what's good for me, I am fortified with knowledge about nutritious foods.

_____
(child's name)

PEANUT BUTTER

Gobble Gobble Award
Presented to

_____
(child's name)

THANKSGIVING

December

Theme	Monday	Tuesday	Wednesday	Thursday	Friday
Winter	Winter White Day	Make ice castles	Snowflake hunt	Sock skating party	Cooking Day: Snowballs
Winter	Bring in a picture of a Winter sport	Snow Play Day	Build a snowperson	Bring in a scarf to share	Cooking Day: Snow
Christmas Around the World	Piñata Hit (Mexico)	Leave out shoes to be filled with candy (France)	Make a gift for a friend (Germany)	Boxing Day: Give a gift to a public servant (England)	Cooking Day: Kutya (Russia)
Winter Holidays	Winter Solstice parade	Kwanzaa feast	Rosa Parks Day	Hanukkah celebration	Cooking Day: Potato Latkes

Extra Days

Extra Day: Wear something that protects us from the cold	Extra Day: Bring in wrapping paper from a Christmas present	Extra Day: Make New Year resolutions

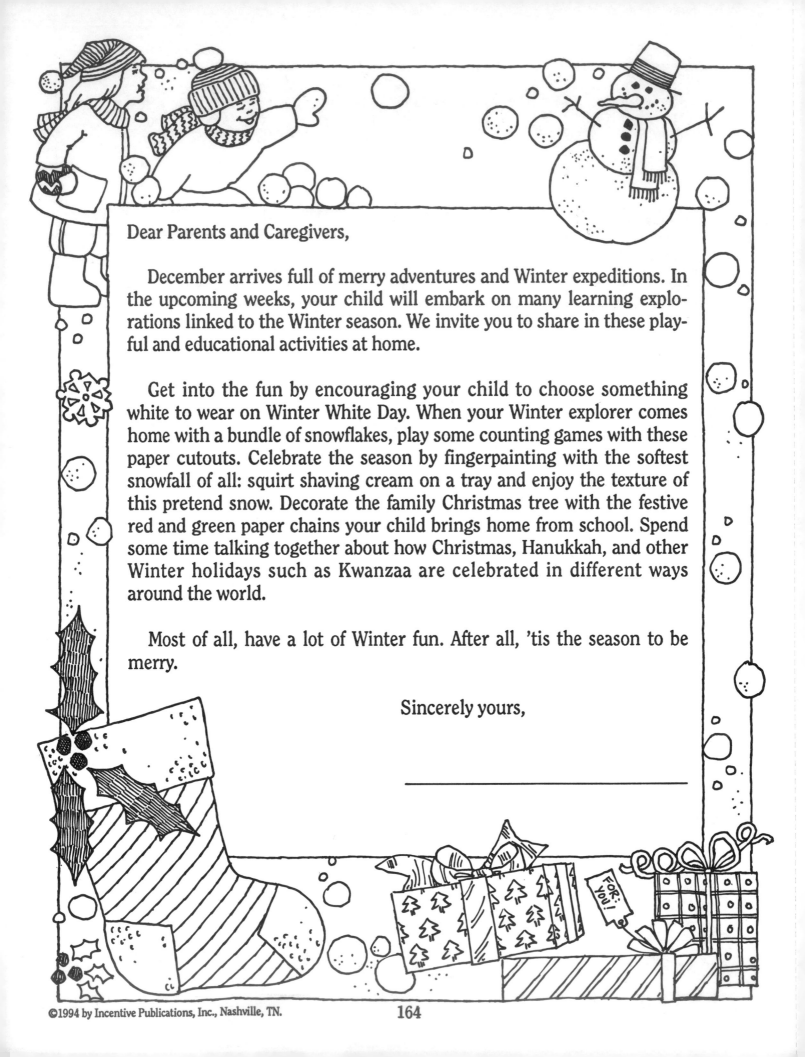

Dear Parents and Caregivers,

December arrives full of merry adventures and Winter expeditions. In the upcoming weeks, your child will embark on many learning explorations linked to the Winter season. We invite you to share in these playful and educational activities at home.

Get into the fun by encouraging your child to choose something white to wear on Winter White Day. When your Winter explorer comes home with a bundle of snowflakes, play some counting games with these paper cutouts. Celebrate the season by fingerpainting with the softest snowfall of all: squirt shaving cream on a tray and enjoy the texture of this pretend snow. Decorate the family Christmas tree with the festive red and green paper chains your child brings home from school. Spend some time talking together about how Christmas, Hanukkah, and other Winter holidays such as Kwanzaa are celebrated in different ways around the world.

Most of all, have a lot of Winter fun. After all, 'tis the season to be merry.

Sincerely yours,

_____

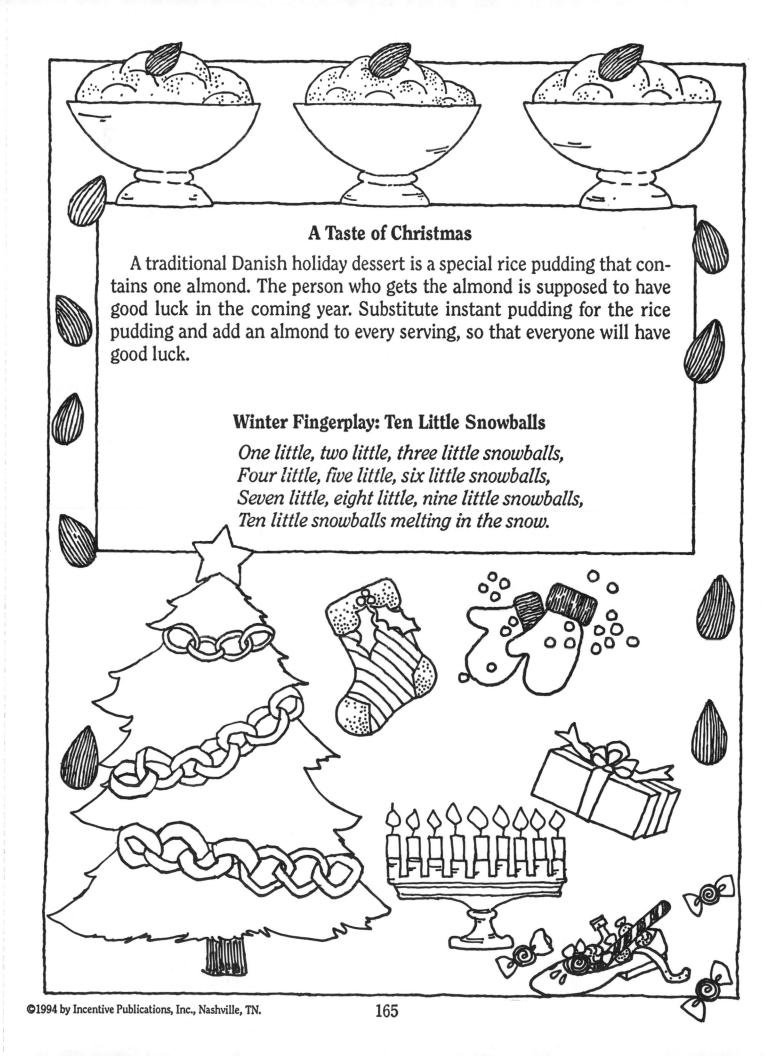

A Taste of Christmas

A traditional Danish holiday dessert is a special rice pudding that contains one almond. The person who gets the almond is supposed to have good luck in the coming year. Substitute instant pudding for the rice pudding and add an almond to every serving, so that everyone will have good luck.

Winter Fingerplay: Ten Little Snowballs

One little, two little, three little snowballs,
Four little, five little, six little snowballs,
Seven little, eight little, nine little snowballs,
Ten little snowballs melting in the snow.

DECEMBER

Week 1: Winter

Facts

- Winter is the coldest season of the year in the Northern Hemisphere. This season begins in the middle of December and ends in the middle of March.
- The cold months of the year are often regarded as dreary since many plants become dormant. Green grass turns brown, and most trees lose their leaves.
- The cold weather brings snow, ice storms, frozen lakes and streams, and icicles.
- People need to protect themselves from the cold by wearing warm clothing and staying indoors.

Special Days

Monday: To introduce your study of Winter, have children wear white clothes to match the color of snow.

Tuesday: Freeze water that has been placed in many different-sized containers. Bring the frozen water outside for children to use to build ice castles. Children pile the ice blocks vertically and horizontally, using salt to help the blocks stick together.

Wednesday: Each child cuts a snowflake shape from white construction paper by folding a piece of paper in half and cutting out jagged edges. After the snowflakes have been made, throw them in the air and have children try to catch them as they fall down.

Thursday: Children pretend their tile or wooden floor is an outdoor frozen pond. Invite them to take off their shoes and ice skate on the pond.

Friday: Taste Snowballs at snacktime (page 167).

Circle Time

1. Create a Winter scene on a piece of newsprint. Use a twig to represent a tree in the Winter and cotton balls to represent snow. Add a frozen pond made from blue construction paper. As you are constructing the mural, discuss with children how they would dress on a snowy day. Ask them what they would need to wear if they were to go ice skating on the frozen pond. The children may have some ideas of items to add to the Winter scene.
   Winter/Mural

2. Read *The Mitten* at the beginning of Circle Time and then play a mitten match game. Cut out several pairs of mittens from construction paper (use a variety of colors) and put matching designs on each mitten pair. Mix up the pairs and hand one mitten to each child, asking him or her to find its match. A variation on this activity is to create a folder game by gluing half of a set of mitten pairs onto a manila folder. Place the other half of the mittens in a pocket glued on the manila folder. During a free-time activity, children try to pair the mittens in the pocket of the folder with their matches.

If desired, cover the board and game pieces with contact paper or laminate them.
Literature/Matching Game

3. Bring to Circle Time a bowl of ice cubes. Children put ice cubes on their hands, noses, cheeks, arms, etc., and tell how it feels. Allow children to experiment by placing the ice cubes on their clothing. Point out how different the ice cubes feel against bare skin. Discuss how being cold feels.
    Observation/Sense of Touch

4. Gather a variety of pine cones of different sizes and shapes. Children pass the pine cones around, noting the different texture and weight of each pine cone. At the culmination of the activity, have children line up the pine cones according to size.
    Observation/Sense of Touch/Size Recognition

Art Activities

Snowperson: Provide each child with three circles of different sizes cut from white construction paper. These circles will form the body of the snowperson. Children build their snowpeople and glue them onto sheets of blue construction paper. They can decorate their snowpeople with beans, raisins, red hots, and buttons.

Snow-Covered Pine Cone: Children dab the tips of pine cones in white tempera paint. For an extra-special touch, mix glitter with the white paint.

Winter Scenery: Cut out small pine tree shapes from green construction paper and distribute one to each child. Children glue their trees to pieces of black construction paper and dip toothbrushes in white paint to brush onto the paper and the trees.

Snow Painting: Children fingerpaint using shaving cream that has been sprayed on a table top or plastic tray.

Tasty Treats

Snowballs: A peeled apple looks like a white snowball. Peel one for each child. Have fun eating the peels, too.

Slushies: Freeze fruit juice in ice cube trays. Once frozen, place ice cubes in a blender and mix until slushy.

Books: Winter

The Jacket I Wear in the Snow by Shirley Neitzel. Scholastic, 1989.

Katy and the Big Snow by Virginia Lee Burton. Houghton, 1943.

The Mitten adapted and illustrated by Jan Brett. Scholastic, 1989.

Snow Day by Betsy Maestro. Scholastic, 1989.

Winter's Coming by Eve Bunting. Harcourt Brace Jovanovich, 1977.

See page 175 for Winter Certificate.

DECEMBER

Week 2: Winter

Special Days

Monday: Children share pictures of Winter sports (skiing, snow sledding, ice skating, ice hockey, etc.).

Tuesday: Read the book *The Snowy Day* and bring children outside to enjoy the Winter weather. If there is snow in your area, let children delight in its texture by packing and throwing snowballs. If there is no snow in your area, contact your local packing company for a donation of crushed ice. Children will have no trouble pretending it is real snow.

Wednesday: If there is snow on the ground, take children outside to construct snowpeople. If there is no snow, try to construct snowpeople from tumbleweeds of various sizes and shapes that have been painted white. For finishing touches, add hats and construction paper eyes, noses, and mouths.

Thursday: Children bring to school scarves of various colors and patterns.

Friday: Make Snow for snacktime (page 169).

Circle Time

1. Bring to Circle Time a variety of Winter clothing and some Winter sports equipment (such as ice skates or skis). Add a few articles of Summer clothing to the pile and ask children to decide which articles of clothing are appropriate for Winter weather. A good follow-up activity is skiing on blocks. Place two long, flat blocks on a carpeted floor. Children stand on the blocks and move their feet to ski across the floor.
   Winter Clothing/Gross Motor Activity

2. Cut ten icicles from white tagboard. Add silver glitter to give them a special holiday look. Put the icicles on a small tray and pass them around the circle. Ask each child to count out a specified number of icicles.
   Math/Counting

3. Children think of ways they can stay warm during the Winter months. Make a list of all ideas and have children add to the list each day. Some ideas include wearing a jacket, sitting by a fireplace, staying indoors, etc.
   Brainstorming

4. Bring a table tennis ball to Circle Time and pretend it is a snowball. As children are sitting in a circle, they roll the ball to each other, saying the person's name at which they direct the ball. Accompany this activity with the following fingerplay:

   ### Ten Little Snowballs

   One little, two little, three little snowballs,
   Four little, five little, six little snowballs,
   Seven little, eight little, nine little snowballs,
   Ten little snowballs melting in the snow.

   Gross Motor Activity/Language Development

Art Activities

White on Black: Each child folds a piece of black construction paper in half and then reopens it. A small amount of white tempera paint is then placed in the middle of the crease, and the paper is folded once again. When their papers are opened, children will see a snowperson, icicle, snow storm, etc.

Snowperson: Each child rolls play dough into balls to build a snowperson. Beads can be used for the nose and eyes, sticks can be used for arms, and fabric scraps can be used to represent a scarf.

Skier: Each child glues two popsicle sticks (to represent a pair of skis) on a piece of construction paper and then draws a skier on the pair of skis.

Tasty Treats

Snow: Crush ice and add fruit juice for flavor. Serve in small bowls to children.

Stone Soup To Warm the Bones: Read *Stone Soup* before preparing your real soup. Mix water with two chicken bullion cubes and add fresh vegetables suggested by the children.

Books: Winter

Jingle Bells by Maryann Kovalski. Little, Brown and Company, 1988.

The Snowy Day by Ezra Jack Keats. Viking Press, 1962.

The Winter Bear by Ruth Craft. Atheneum, 1974.

The Winter Noisy Book by Margaret Wise Brown. Harper and Row, 1947.

See page 175 for Winter Certificate.

Week 3: Christmas Around The World

Facts

- Christmas traditions vary from country to country.
- The children of Amsterdam, Denmark, believe that Saint Nicholas rides a horse over their rooftops and leaves presents. In Denmark, Christmas is a two-day celebration, occurring on December 25th and 26th. Christmas trees are decorated with apples and a star on top.
- Christmas in Mexico is celebrated with posadas (inns), parades, and piñatas. For nine evenings before Christmas, friends gather in parades, carrying candles and singing Christmas carols as they pretend to walk to the inn where Jesus was born in Bethlehem. Each night of the posada (the walk to the inn), children play piñata, a game in which children are blindfolded and attempt to hit a piñata that has been stuffed with either water, confetti, or candy and toys.

DECEMBER

- St. Lucia Day begins the Christmas celebration in Sweden. St. Lucia lived during the 4th century A.D., a time when many Christians were persecuted for their religious beliefs. Lucia carried food to Christians hiding in tunnels, and it is said that she wore candles on her head to light her way. Today, St. Lucia Day is celebrated in Sweden by the eldest girl in the family carrying coffee and buns to her family members. She is supposed to dress in white and wear an evergreen wreath with seven lighted candles to symbolize the passage of St. Lucia.

Special Days

Monday: Purchase a piñata and fill it with popcorn, raisins, and peanuts. Children are blindfolded and take turns trying to hit the piñata. Allow children to share the treats inside the piñata.

Tuesday: Have children set out their shoes to be filled with candy. This custom originated in France, where children hope that Pére Noel will fill their shoes with presents.

Wednesday: Today, children make cards and pictures for their friends in the German tradition of giving special gifts to their loved ones at Christmas.

Thursday: On Boxing Day, English children make gifts to give to public servants. Today, have children do the same. Some suggestions include cereal bracelets and necklaces or tree ornaments made from beads strung on pipe cleaners.

Friday: Prepare the Russian desert kutya (page 171).

Circle Time

1. Attach a large Christmas tree cut from newsprint to the wall. Children paint the tree green and decorate it with handmade ornaments. Children can make their own ornaments by decorating circles cut from construction paper with sequins, beads, glitter, markers, etc. Ask children to tell why they chose to decorate their ornaments as they did. After the ornaments have been attached to the tree, ask children to count them. Write each child's name by his or her ornament. This helps with name recognition as each child tries to find his or her ornament throughout the week.
   Art/Counting/Name Recognition

2. Tell the children the story of St. Lucia. Ask children to pretend they are living in Sweden and to act out the St. Lucia celebration. Provide a paper evergreen wreath with paper candles glued on top for a prop.
   Christmas Custom/Sweden/Acting Out

3. Cut a large Christmas tree from green construction paper and hang it on a wall near your Circle Time area. Count the days until Christmas by placing a star on the tree each day.
   Counting/Math

4. Explain to the children that it is a Christmas tradition in Iraq to light a fire, let the flames die out, and then jump over the ashes three times while making a wish. Set out some sticks for a pretend fire and have each child participate in this custom. Discuss everyone's wishes after the game is over.
   Christmas Custom/Iraq/Gross Motor Activity/Communication

5. In the Spanish Christmas tradition, each child writes his or her name on a slip of paper. After all of the names have been placed in a jar, someone draws the names out, two at a time. It is said that each pair of names will be best friends during the upcoming year. Have each pair of children play a game or work on a project together.
Christmas Custom/Spain/Cooperative Learning

Art Activities

St. Lucia's Evergreen Wreath: Cut a paper headband from green paper and glue small pine cones to its side. Cut seven paper candles from white construction paper and glue around the top of the headband.

Amsterdam Christmas Tree: Children cut out Christmas tree shapes from green construction paper and decorate their trees with red apples and yellow stars.

Luminaries: Distribute a small paper bag to each child. Instruct the children to fill their bags half-way to the top with sand. The teacher or an assistant should place a candle into each bag, light the candles, and place the bags around the room (out of reach of children!). This is a Mexican Christmas tradition.

Chinese Paper Lanterns: Fold a piece of construction paper lengthwise and make cuts in the fold with scissors. Open the paper and roll and staple together its short ends. Make a handle from a strip of construction paper. Staple the handle to one of the ends and hang with a piece of yarn.

Tasty Treats

Kutya: Prepare a hot wheat cereal, adding to it raisins and honey.

Cinnamon Buns for St. Lucia: Distribute frozen bread dough (enough for one bun) to each child. Children knead and roll out the dough, sprinkling it with brown sugar, cinnamon, and raisins. Top with a pat of butter and bake according to package directions.

Denmark Desert: At Christmas, Danish people make a special rice pudding into which one almond is added. The person who receives the almond in his or her serving will have good luck during the upcoming year. Substitute instant pudding (any flavor) for the rice pudding and add an almond to each serving.

Books: Christmas Around the World

The Berenstain Bears' Christmas Tree by Stan and Jan Berenstain. Random House, 1980.

Clifford's Christmas by Norman Bridwell. Scholastic, 1984.

Happy Christmas Gemma by Sarah Hayes. Lothrop, Lee & Shepard, 1986.

Little Bear's Christmas by Janice Brustlein. Lothrop, Lee & Shepard, 1984.

Merry Christmas Mom and Dad by Mercer Mayer. Western Publishing Co., 1982.

See page 176 for Christmas Around the World Certificate.

Week 4: Winter Holidays

Facts

- The Winter Solstice marks the official start of Winter. The Winter Solstice occurs about December 22 when the Sun is in the southernmost part of the sky, bringing to the Northern Hemisphere the shortest day of the year. Festivals to honor the Sun are celebrated in all parts of the world with the burning of bonfires, logs, and candles.

- Kwanzaa (Fresh Fruit) is a holiday observed by some African-American families. It is a week-long celebration that begins on Christmas Day and commemorates the African Harvest. Rituals that symbolize togetherness are celebrated throughout the week. These include candle lighting (mishummas), unity cup (kikombe), and parties with gift-giving each day. New Year's Day brings a harvest feast which emphasizes the unity of the family.

- Hanukkah (also called Chanukah or the Festival of Lights) is an 8-day Jewish holiday occurring about the same time as Christmas. It celebrates the Hebrew people's religious freedom from the Syrian Greeks in 165 B.C. Upon winning their religious freedom, the Jewish people wanted to purify their temple before worshipping there. When it was time to light the temple, it was discovered that there was only enough oil to burn for one day; however, according to the Talmud, a miracle occurred. Once lit, that one jar of oil burned for eight days. Today Jewish families celebrate this miracle by lighting a candle in the menorah for each of the eight days of Hanukkah.

- One day in December of 1955, a brave African-American woman named Rosa Parks sat in a front seat of a Montgomery, Alabama, city bus. At the time, the front seats of all public buses were reserved for white people. African-Americans were made to sit at the backs of buses. Rosa Parks, who was tired after a day at work, made a decision to sit in an empty front seat rather than stand for lack of an empty back seat. Her decision got her arrested. As a result of her action, however, African-Americans refused to ride the buses until they were no longer segregated. This is an example of a nonviolent protest action that helped bring about the civil rights movement.

Special Days

Monday: Celebrate the Winter Solstice with a parade. Decorate a tree with red construction paper berries and parade around your room or school holding homemade candles (see page 173 for instructions).

Tuesday: Begin your Kwanzaa feast by giving each child a mkeka (mat). If you have carpet squares available you may use them as your mats. Have each child sit on a mkeka and cut and distribute mazao (fruits and vegetables) to each child.

Wednesday: Ask each child to bring to class a picture that represents his or her own concept of freedom to celebrate Rosa Parks Day. Some ideas include the right to live anywhere one chooses, to play in any park one chooses, to drink from any available drinking fountain, etc.

DECEMBER

Thursday: Ask each child to bring to school a candle to be lit for the menorah. Let children share their candles and discuss the differences in size and color of each candle.

Friday: Cook Potato Latkes for a snack (page 174).

Circle Time

1. Introduce the Winter Solstice and discuss the importance of the Sun to all life forms. Ask the children how the Sun makes them feel and what they like about the Sun. Ask them to discuss ways the Sun can be harmful, as well.
   Science/Communication

2. Place a piece of newsprint on the floor and draw the outline of a bus. Children can add the wheels, windows, and people. Ask the group whether or not they like riding on a bus and whether or not riding on a school bus makes them anxious. Ask them how they might feel if they were allowed to ride only in the back of the bus because of the color of their eyes, hair, or skin?
   Communication/Feelings/Social & Racial Issues

3. Pass a Unity Cup (use a coffee cup or paper cup), as is done during the holiday of Kwanzaa. Discuss the idea of bringing unity to the group.
   Communication/Feelings

4. Make or purchase a driedel to bring to Circle Time. Explain to children what the letters on each side of the driedel mean: the N stands for Nothing, the G stands for All, the H stands for Half, and the S means Put It. Supply each child with 10 pennies, raisins, peanuts, etc. At the start of the game, each child places one object in the center of the circle. The driedel is then spun by each child, who either wins or loses pieces according to the spin of the top.
   Hanukkah Custom/Following Directions/Counting

5. Make eight small candles, one large candle, and nine flames from construction paper. Collect small gifts to be given to the children (e.g. cereal box prizes, note pads, crayons, etc.) and explain that Hanukkah is celebrated for eight days by lighting a candle and giving a gift on each day. Celebrate in your classroom by asking a different child to pretend to light one of the smaller candles with the large candle by placing the flame on top of the candle. Pass out gifts to each child after each candle has been lit.
   Hanukkah Custom/Menorah

Art Activities

Candles: Children paint toilet paper rolls various bright colors to represent candles. Red construction paper flames can be placed on the tops of the candles.

Kwanzaa Flags: Supply each child with a rectangular piece of white paper onto which a tongue depressor has been attached. Children decorate their flags using red, green, and black crayons.

Sunshine Art: Cut circles from yellow construction paper to represent the Sun. Give a Sun shape and a blank sheet of paper to each child to create an individual piece of art.

DECEMBER

Unity Mat: Place corn (muhindi) and other vegetables and fruit (mazao) on a unity mat (mkeka). Each child can make his or her own unity mat by cutting a fringe or scalloped border around the edges of a sheet of construction paper. Precut pictures of fruits and vegetables are then glued onto the mat. If desired, the teacher can trace actual pieces of fruit onto pieces of paper for children to cut out. The unity mat symbolizes the firm foundation of love and respect a household must have to endure.

Tasty Treats

Candy Tree: Place a sugar cone upside-down and spread with green frosting. For decoration, add red cinnamon candies to the frosting.

Potato Latkes:
- 1 onion, grated
- 1 teaspoon salt
- 1 egg
- 6 medium-sized potatoes, washed, pared, grated
- 3 tablespoons flour
- ½ teaspoon baking powder

Add the onion, salt, and egg to the potatoes and beat well. Mix together remaining ingredients and beat into potato mixture. Drop by spoonfuls into hot oil. Brown on both sides. Drain. Serve with applesauce or sour cream.

Muhindi (Corn): In some areas of Africa, one ear of muhindi is placed on the mkeka (mat) to symbolize each child in the family. Cook corn with the children and discuss how many children are in each of their families.

Books: Winter Holidays

I Love Hanukkah by Marilyn Hirsh. Holiday, 1984.

It's Chanukah! by Ellie Gellman. Kar Ben, 1985.

Kwanzaa by Deborah M. Newton Chocolate. Children's Press, 1990.

Kwanzaa by A. P. Porter. Carolrhoda Books, Inc., 1991.

My First Kwanzaa Book by Deborah M. Newton Chocolate. Scholastic, 1992.

See page 176 for Winter Holidays Certificate.

Winter

I explored the
Wonders
of
Winter.

My name is: _____

WINTER

I read and learned about skiing, sledding, skating, scarves, soup, and snow!

My name is: _____

CHRISTMAS

I learned how Christmas is celebrated in many different ways around the world.

My name is:

_____

AROUND THE WORLD

WINTER

I discovered that Winter holidays are celebrated in many different ways.

My name is:

_____

HOLIDAYS